A WALKING TOUR OF

HISTORIC FRANKFORT

To Mitch and Lisa
Moore
We hope you enjoy this
stroll through one of one
Kentucky's greatest towns!,

Russell Hatter

Gene Burch

A Walking Tour
of Historic Frankfort

Second printing 2003

TEXT: Russell Hatter
PHOTOGRAPHY: Gene Burch
GRAPHIC DESIGN: Paul Neff Design, Cincinnati, Ohio

ISBN: 0-9637008-3-9

Manufactured in China

A WALKING TOUR OF
HISTORIC FRANKFORT

TEXT BY **RUSSELL HATTER**

PHOTOGRAPHS BY **GENE BURCH**

Acknowledgements

It is reasonable to believe you purchased this book because of the photographs. The contribution of Gene Burch's photography is a beautiful tribute to those who have lived in these historic houses. I feel confident they would be as pleased with the representations as I am. Without these special images, this work would have been incomplete and probably overlooked.

I owe a great debt of thanks to graphic design artist Paul Neff of Cincinnati. Not just for his expertise and suggestions, but his patience with last minute changes and the frustrations of a first-time writer.

My wife, Karen Kimmel, has been a tremendous support during two years of writing. I cannot thank her enough for responding to my constant grammatical questions and her readiness to assist when the computer intimidated me.

Without the research and writings of those who came before me, it would have been impossible to share this information. Their names are found in the bibliography. A special thanks goes to the Thomas C. Clark Library at the Kentucky History Center, the Kentucky Heritage Commission, the Kentucky Library and Archives, the University Press of Kentucky and the Frankfort-Franklin County Tourist and Convention Commission. I must thank the Kentucky Historical Society's Curator of Rare Books, Ron Bryant. His knowledge, his joy in sharing information and his love for history have been an inspiration to me.

There have been others who have contributed to this work, and I apologize if you do not find your name listed. Bob Arnold, Judy Bailey, Teresa Barton, Barney Bernard, Chuck Bogart, Mariam Burge, Susan Brown, Barri Christian, Larry Cleveland, Pat Cockerill, William Coffee, Nash Cox, William Crumbaugh, Brenda Duvall, Charles Ellestad, Helen Evans, Tom Fugate, Skip Gaines, Danny Garland, Kenny Goin, John Gray, Sara Harger, Ken Hart, Mike Hawkins, Mike Haynes, Steve Henry, David Hilton, David Hinson, Billy Mack Hoge, Nicky Hughes, Susan Lyons Hughes, Joedy Isert, William E. Johnson, Patrick Kennedy, Patty Kimmel, William Kirkland, Alison Kissling, Trudy Laing, Lane Lewis, Sam McNamara, Judy Markwell, Corky Mohedano, Martha Moore, Roy Nance, Mark Overstreet, Jack Palmer, Bryant Peavler, Bob Polsgrove, Jim Richardson, Roberta Roberts, Paula Rutledge, John Ryan, Leila W. Salisbury, Jean Davis Shaw, Frank Sower, Richard Taylor, John M. Trowbridge, Cathy West, and Wilma Yeary.

About the photographs…

The photographs for this book were taken with a Nikon N90S, Canon EOS3, and a Sony DSC F707 5.2 megapixel digital camera. Both Fuji Velvia slide film and Kodak 100 Gold negative file were used in the conventional cameras. All the film was scanned using the Nikon Coolscan 4000ED film scanner and the images color corrected in Adobe Photoshop 7.0. The only digital manipulations other than color and contrast corrections were the occasional removal of objectionable utility lines.

   I would like to thank Russ Hatter for inviting me to take the photos for this project. The concept for this book was conceived on one of our several hiking trips in the Red River Gorge. Hopefully, now that it is finished, we can resume our trips back there.

   I would like to thank my wife, Mary Ann, my children, and my dental co-workers for their patience as I toiled with this project. Thanks also to Bob Lanham of Lanham Media Services for his expert advice on image selection and the four-color printing process.

   Gene Burch

CONTENTS

HISTORIC FRANKFORT
Today and Yesterday

During Kentucky's bicentennial in 1992 Pegasus Players, a local theatre group, received a state grant to develop a walking tour of downtown Frankfort, celebrating Frankfort's rich heritage and historic personalities. From this effort has grown an annual summer stroll that tourists and local populace flock to enjoy. The original tour ran about an hour, but as more information was gathered about Frankfort over the years, the walk became longer than the average person wanted to take. That was the impetus for this book, to allow readers to learn about Kentucky's capital at their own leisure and to walk the area at their own pace.

This is a guide to Frankfort's past, a look at the architecture and the people who contributed to today's Frankfort. It is a street-by-street view of north Frankfort's past, and through the photography of Gene Burch, a look at the present. At least the way we were in the year 2002.

Each chapter consists of an individual street with selected information relative to the history, the people, and the architecture of the buildings. It is not necessary to begin with the first chapter or to read the chapters in any specific order. No matter how you take your tour— by page, on foot, or in your car— it is our hope that you will find a deeper pride in and appreciation of Frankfort, Kentucky's capital city.

Chapter One
WAPPING STREET

Wapping Street runs east and west parallel to the Kentucky River. The name Wapping comes from "Wapping Old Stair,"
the King's wharf in London. Local historian Nettie Glenn writes that the street was named by John Instone, a homesick
Englishman who claimed the area reminded him of London's old Wapping on the Thames that John Stow had described
in 1605: "Here was the Execution Block, the usual place for hanging of pirates and rovers at low water mark and there
to remain until three tides had overflowed them." Instone had a dwelling on Wapping Street and was a friend of and
boat-builder for Frankfort's founder James Wilkinson.

The Old Post Office CIRCA 1887 — 305 WAPPING STREET

Before this Romanesque Revival style building became the home of Frankfort's library, it housed the post office and
the federal court, erected on the original site of Saffell's Valley Mill at the corner of St. Clair and Wapping Streets. On April 20,1882,
President Chester A. Arthur signed a congressional appropriation bill authorizing one hundred thousand dollars for construction of
the federal building. Bedford limestone was used and a 60-foot tower with cupola was centered over the front entrance. The building
was open for public use by 1887. In 1910 a rear wing was added under the direction of James Knox Taylor, supervising architect for
the United States Treasury Department. With the construction of a new post office in the mid-1960s and the John C. Watts Federal
Building in 1975, the building became a permanent library location. At the time, the library was managed by the Frankfort Woman's
Club at their offices in the former ante-bellum home of Governor Robert P. Letcher on the northwest corner of Washington and
Wapping Streets. During an extensive renovation of the federal building, the library was moved to a temporary location at Fountain
Place in the Capital Plaza. It was rededicated as the permanent home of the Paul Sawyier Library on August 15, 1976. As the library
expanded services they outgrew this building and in the spring of 2002 plans were made to build a new structure in the adjacent
parking lot. Frankfort City Hall was exploring moving into the old library building.

Paul Sawyier is Frankfort's most celebrated artist. He was born March 23, 1865, at Table Rock in Madison County,
Ohio. At age five his parents, Dr. Nathaniel and Ellen Wingate Sawyier, moved to Ellen's hometown of Frankfort. They lived across from

the railroad depot on Broadway where the Kentucky History Center now stands. He received training from nationally known oil portrait painter Frank Duveneck in Cincinnati, and studied under William Merrit Chase in New York City. He worked for a time as a sales representative for his father at the Kentucky River Mills in Frankfort, but nothing really satisfied him except his painting. He painted many scenes of Frankfort, Franklin County, and the Kentucky River, where he lived for several years on a houseboat. He moved to New York where he would later die of a heart attack at age 52 on November 5, 1917. In 1923 he was re-interred in the Frankfort cemetery.

Sawyier created an estimated three thousand sketches, oils and watercolors, many of which hang on the walls of Frankfort homes and businesses. Several books have been written about his life and work: *Paul Sawyier: American Artist* by Willard Rouse Jillson; the historical novel *Love to All, Your Paul* by Nettie Glenn; Arthur F. Jones' *The Art of Paul Sawyier* and Mary Michele Hainel's *A Kentucky Artist: Paul Sawyier.*

J. J. King was a close friend and patron of Sawyier. King's collection of his artwork was often on display in Frankfort. During the 1960s part of the King collection was displayed in an art show sponsored by the Frankfort Jaycees. From this event, the Paul Sawyier Galleries formed in 1968. William Coffey became the sole owner of the Galleries in 1981. Sawyier's paintings are auctioned in Louisville, Lexington, and even at Sotheby's in New York. Today original paintings by Paul Sawyier range in price from $1,500 to $20,000. Sawyier was a prolific painter. Even today long lost paintings and sketches are still turning up. His work is not only a pleasure to the eye, but also an important contribution to the history of Frankfort in the latter 1800s and early 1900s.

Good Shepherd Parish CIRCA 1850 — 310 WAPPING STREET

Born in 1810, Father James Madison Lancaster was the first resident pastor of Good Shepherd Parish. He came from a prominent family and at his father's death inherited a sizable estate. Before he arrived in Frankfort he served two years as Vice President at St. Joseph's College and one year as pastor of St. Joseph's Cathedral in Bardstown, Kentucky.

When he came to Frankfort in 1848, the church was using a small dwelling on High Street near the present railroad tunnel. The church had been meeting under the direction of member Ellen Barstow in various Frankfort locations since 1835. Mass was first said regularly across from the Old Capitol on the southeast corner of St. Clair and Broadway. For a time members met in what was called the "tunnel house," next to the railroad tunnel on High Street. In a search for adequate space, Lancaster bought the Presbyterian Church and parsonage on Wapping Street. The property was purchased for $5000 and conveyed to the Catholic Church in the name of James M. Lancaster. The Sisters of Charity of Nazareth, in the adjacent building, received the deed to the parsonage. In 1850 Father Lancaster began construction of a new building. The Presbyterian Church building remained intact and the Catholic congregation used it for worship services while the new building was finished. The parishioners performed most of the work on their own time. The Gothic church building was built around and over the former Presbyterian structure and when nearly completed, the old church was razed from within. Parish member John Haly, who constructed many of Frankfort's downtown buildings, assisted in much of the work.

In 1922, an architect from Covington, a Mr. Crowe, constructed the present adjacent school building for over $70,000 including the cost of the lot. The building was dedicated in August 1923.

During the Civil War, Transylvania student Thomas Major joined John Hunt Morgan's band of Confederate raiders. During Morgan's raid into Ohio, Major was captured and imprisoned in the Columbus penitentiary. After a daring escape where Morgan and others tunneled beneath the prison walls, Major was wounded and again captured. During incarceration, he fell deathly ill and it was only through the ministrations of Catholic nuns that he became whole. Due to the kindness of those nuns, following the war Major became a priest and came to serve at the Good Shepherd Parish in 1895. Just before he died in 1911, he baptized a baby who eventually became a community leader and mayor of Frankfort. In the year 1910, on the tenth day of December, at ten minutes past ten, Reverend Major baptized a ten pound, ten ounce baby boy: Frank W. Sower.

Reverend Thomas Major is buried in the Frankfort Cemetery.

In the year 1910, on the tenth day of December, at ten minutes past ten, Reverend Major baptized a ten pound, ten ounce baby boy who would become mayor of Frankfort: Frank W. Sower.

Thomas Todd House

Thomas Todd House CIRCA 1812 — 320 WAPPING STREET

United States Supreme Court Justice Thomas Todd purchased this house from its builder, either Hayden Edwards or William Waller, in 1818. The original house did not have the Victorian look we see today. Edwards (or Waller) built a Federal style dwelling that did not have the three gables, the gingerbread trim, or the covered front porch. These features were added later. In 1945 Good Shepherd Church bought the house at auction and it became a convent for the Sisters of Charity. Forty years later Don and Toni Wood bought the property and donated it to the First United Methodist Church in memory of Mr. Wood's parents, Clinton and Edith Wood. This building now houses church offices, the minister's study, a library, classrooms, and a dining room.

From a specially prepared booklet on the history of the house, we learn that the bricks used in 1812 were hand-made and placed on the ground to dry in the sun. On some of the bricks can be seen the prints of goats and chickens that walked across them. The house contained a basement, entrance hall, the front four rooms of the first floor, and the front three rooms on the second floor. The ash floors on the first level are original to the house. The plaster is also original and contains hog-hair bristles and horsehair commonly used in the 1800s to bond plaster together. The two two-story wings were added over 100 years ago. The front door, the beautiful fanlight and the door lock are original, as is the stairway with cherry banister in the entry hall.

The Todd House chimney system is unique. The parlor fireplace shares a flue with fireplaces in the dining room and the second floor. At each end of the house, flues from the first floor fireplaces run vertically, then make right angle turns toward each other and join the flue of the fireplace upstairs.

Thomas Todd was born January 23, 1765, in King and Queen County, Virginia. His father died when Thomas was only eighteen months old. Beginning at age fourteen, he served several enlistments in the Continental Army during the Revolutionary War. Following his service in the war he lived with his mother's relative, Harry Innis, and studied law and land surveying. In 1783 Innis was appointed Judge of the District Court for the newly created District of Kentucky in Virginia. In 1789 Judge Innis appointed Todd a clerk in his court. When Kentucky held its conventions seeking separation from Virginia, Todd was selected as the secretary. Kentucky attained statehood in 1792 and Todd was appointed Clerk of the Court of Appeals, the first to hold that office. In 1806 he became Chief Justice and was later appointed Associate Justice of the Supreme Court by President Thomas Jefferson. After his first wife Elizabeth Harris died, in 1811 he married Mrs. Lucy Payne Washington, the sister of the celebrated Dolly Madison, wife of President James Madison. Their marriage took place in the East Room of the White House, the first celebrated in the presidential mansion. Lafayette met with Mrs. Todd here on his famous tour of the United States in 1825. Thomas Todd died February 7, 1826 and was buried in the family graveyard of his mentor and friend Harry Innis. Todd and his wife were re-interred later in the Frankfort Cemetery.

Kentucky's first native born governor, James T. Morehead and his wife, lived here with Mrs. Todd after her husband's death. Morehead was born in 1797 just five years after Kentucky became a state. When Morehead's wife died, he moved for a short time to the Charles Morehead house on the northeast corner of Main and Washington Streets. Elected Lieutenant Governor in 1832, J. T. Morehead became governor on the death of Governor John Breathitt in 1834. He had an excellent library, embracing one of the largest collections of Kentucky histories at that time. A very small and inexpensive monument marks his grave in the Frankfort Cemetery.

Vest-Lindsey House CIRCA 1798 — 401 WAPPING STREET

This is one of the oldest houses in Frankfort, possibly constructed around 1798 by Lexington businessman Andrew Holmes. (Some accounts say it was built by Alexander Macey in 1816 or Littleberry Bachelor in 1831.) During restoration of the house in the 1960s, Dr. Willard Rouse Jillson discovered the initials "A H 1798" scratched on a rafter in the west end of the attic. Although he was not a resident of Frankfort, Holmes was extremely instrumental in the town becoming the capital of Kentucky. In 1786, Revolutionary War General James Wilkinson founded Frankfort as a local trade center, but the town was slow to develop. Wilkinson solved his indebtedness by selling his local property to Holmes in early 1792. Months later, when Frankfort was considered for the capital of the state, Holmes offered several town lots, rents from a tobacco warehouse, building materials, and $3000 in specie backed by local citizens. The offer was accepted, and construction on a statehouse located on the Public Square began.

The house was originally Federal in style but over the years has taken on many Victorian features. In the early 1960s it was threatened with demolition when a Louisville business firm wanted to erect a three-story state office building on the site. Former Kentucky first lady, Ida Lee Willis, wife of Governor Simeon P. Willis, met with then-Governor Ned Breathitt to save the historic structure. The effort resulted in the creation of the Capital City Heritage Commission, whose charge was to maintain the preservation and development of the Corner in Celebrities area. The plan for the state office building was accepted, but not at the expense of the Vest-Lindsey house. Instead, the Bush Building was built at the rear of the historic site. In honor of Ida Lee Willis and her battle for preservation, there is a lovely memorial garden adjacent to the old home. The Ida Lee Willis Memorial Foundation annually presents awards to individuals and organizations that have made significant contributions to the preservation of Kentucky's historic buildings. The foundation was chartered in honor of Mrs. Willis, the first director of the Kentucky Heritage Commission.

George Graham Vest was born in the home of his grandfather in south Frankfort at the site of the old YMCA at the southwest end of the "singing bridge." His family later moved here to the Wapping Street dwelling where he spent his boyhood days. After graduating from both Centre College in Danville and Transylvania University in Lexington, he moved to Missouri in 1853 to practice law. During the 1860s he served in the Confederate Congress and was in the United States Senate from Missouri for twenty-five years. He is best remembered for a case in which one man sued another for shooting his dog. Vest won for the plaintiff with an emotional closing to the jury, pointing out that "dog is man's best friend," the origin of this familiar phrase.

In 1846 the residence was sold to prominent attorney and state legislator Thomas Noble Lindsey. During the Civil War, his oldest son, Daniel Weisiger Lindsey, recruited the Twenty-second Kentucky Infantry Regiment and served under General James A. Garfield in eastern Kentucky and West Virginia. He was later with General Grant at Vicksburg. A monument at the Mississippi battlefield attests to his contribution. He became Adjutant General as well as Inspector General in charge of all Kentucky Union Army forces. His adjutant general's report contained the military history of every Union Kentucky officer and soldier who took part in the Civil War. When the Confederates attacked Frankfort in 1864, Lindsey successfully supervised the defense of the city. He was a staunch Republican who took an active interest in the welfare of Frankfort, serving as a member of the city council. Lindsey lived here as a boy and as an adult resided on Second Street facing the Kentucky River at "Rika-Done," Russian for river home.

The founder of Frankfort's public library, Miss Lilian Lindsey, also lived here. She took a course in Library Science at the University of Chicago in 1908. It was here that she collected books and other contributions for what would become Frankfort's first official library. On December 12, 1908, Miss Lindsey and the Frankfort Woman's Club officially opened the library on the seventh floor of the newly built McClure Building at the corner of Main and St. Clair. Later the library would be located in the Old Capitol, then in a building on St. Clair near the end of the bridge. In 1925 the library was housed in the Frankfort Woman's Club Building in the Governor Letcher house at Wapping and Washington Streets.

This house is the "Harringford House" of Robert Burns Wilson's 1900 novel *Until the Day Break*, a title lifted from a line in The Song of Solomon in the Bible. Wilson was a frequent dinner guest at the Lindsey table. He is more famous for his paintings and for the writing of "Remember the Maine", the battle hymn of the Spanish-American War. John Fox, Jr. may have stayed here gathering material and color for his novel *The Little Shepherd of Kingdom Come*, the first book in the United States to sell a million copies.

George Graham Vest originated the familiar phrase "Dog is man's best friend."

Rodman-Hewitt House

CIRCA 1817 — 404 WAPPING STREET

We find in deed-books at the Franklin County Courthouse that James Ware bought this property for $1500 from Daniel and Sarah James in July of 1815. By the time the property transferred to Thomas and Ann Hawkins in December of 1817, there was a house on this site, probably constructed by Ware. The present woodwork and room arrangements are traced to this period. After changing hands several times, the property was under the ownership of attorney Lucas Broadhead, who enlarged the house to its size today, and added the left wing. At the death of Broadhead, his wife would remarry Orlando Brown in 1852. In 1858 the two-story brick house was sold to Dr. Hugh Rodman who improved the property considerably. On January 6, 1859, a son, Hugh Rodman, Jr., was born.

Hugh Rodman Jr. was an honor student in the local schools he attended in the city of his birth. He graduated from the United States Naval Academy in 1880 and began his sea duty five years later, just as steel ships began to replace wooden vessels. At the outbreak of the Spanish American War he was a lieutenant and took an active part in the famous battle of Manila Bay when Admiral Dewey destroyed the power of Spain on May 1, 1898. Rodman was Marine Superintendent during the building of the Panama Canal. When America entered World War I, he was one of the first officers to be commissioned Rear Admiral and was transferred to European waters. Given command of the United States Battleship *Squadron*, he served until the surrender of the German fleet at the end of the war. Following the war, Rodman commanded the newly established U.S. Pacific Fleet. He retired in 1923. In 1937 he was invited to attend the coronation of King George VI and was returned to active duty with the rank of admiral. He died on June 7,1940 and was buried in the Arlington National Cemetery.

At the death of Dr. Hugh Rodman, Sr., the home came into the ownership of Fayette Hewitt. He was an officer in the Confederacy, obtaining the rank of general. He and his brother Virgil resided in this house for almost twenty-five years. In 1867, Governor

The Rodman – Hewitt House

John W. Stevenson appointed Hewitt Quartermaster General of Kentucky. Immediately he began an attempt to recover from the United States government the money owed to the state for Kentucky's expenses in arming and equipping the Union soldiers. He held the post successfully for nine years, served as state auditor three successive terms and retired as president of the State National Bank.

During the Civil War, General Hewitt organized the Confederate mail system and was assistant Adjutant General under Jefferson Davis. He served in the famous First Kentucky Brigade, "the Orphan Brigade," under Generals John C. Breckinridge and Ben Hardin Helm. His men loved him because of his courage and bravery. They teased him that he might be serving on some General's staff rather than being with the ragged cavalry, to which he replied, "I would rather be a captain among these men, sir, than to be general of any other brigade in the army." At the conclusion of the war, Hewitt brought back to Kentucky the Brigade's archives, including twenty volumes of record books, morning ledgers, and thousands of individual orders and reports. These he eventually gave to Ed Porter Thompson* who used them in writing his *History of the First Kentucky Brigade*, one of the first histories of a Confederate organization to appear following the war.

On the night of January 26, 1909, Fayette Hewitt died following a fall in the bathroom at his home in Frankfort. His funeral took place at the Church of Ascension on Washington Street and his body was returned to his native Elizabethtown and buried there.

Ed Porter Thompson lived in south Frankfort on the southwest corner of Third and Shelby Streets.

Carneal-Watson House CIRCA 1855 — 407 WAPPING STREET

Thomas Carneal was one of the founders of Covington, Kentucky. His northern Kentucky home is the oldest brick home in Covington. As a legislator from Kenton County he grew to love the city of Frankfort. In 1854 he purchased the lot next to the Lindseys. It had been used as a garden by the heirs of Lucas Broadhead, Sr. The floor plan for this brick Greek Revival residence had only one level because Carneal suffered from the gout and had difficulty with climbing stairs. Carneal was quite wealthy and often hosted lavish parties here. Soon his son Louis Carneal and his family came to live with him, remaining until the father's death in 1860.

In 1863, Frankfort businessman Philip Swigert bought the house and presented it to his brother-in-law John Watson. Watson's wife, Sally Rodes, was a niece of Cassius Marcellus Clay. Of their children, only Howe Watson and his wife Miss Lottie remained at this home, inheriting the property at the death of his parents. Howe's father John was killed accidentally while getting off a train. Following her children's marriages, and the death of her husband Howe, Miss Lottie decided to sell the home and build a residence behind the property, creating a new street. Her son-in-law, Frank Warfield Clay, suggested she name the street Watson Court.

For a few months during the Civil War, the building served as the headquarters for the military board until relocated to Broadway.

"Gray Gables" (Bibb-Burnley House) CIRCA 1857 — 411 WAPPING STREET

John Bibb was born on October 27, 1789, in Prince Edward County, Virginia. He served as a private in the War of 1812, joining the 4th Kentucky Volunteer Regiment. While living in Logan County he was elected to the state legislature, serving in both Houses, and as a result settled in Frankfort in 1856. It was in the rear of this home that he developed a new variety of lettuce that had a compact head and leaves of single serving size. Today restaurant menus from San Francisco to New York City offer salads made with John Bibb's lettuce. His brother was the famed jurist George Mortimer Bibb who served as Secretary of the Treasury during the administration of President John Tyler.

Bibb's niece, Martha Ann Burnley, better known as "Miss Patty," spent the last fifty years of her life in this house. Because of her cultural interests, Gray Gables became a rendezvous for poets, artists, and musicians. Among them John Fox Jr., who wrote *The Little Shepherd of Kingdom Come*, the first American novel to sell more than a million copies, and Robert Burns Wilson, painter, poet and author of the battle hymn of the Spanish-American War: "Remember, Remember the Maine."

Both Bibb and Miss Patty are buried in the Frankfort Cemetery.

This is also the site of one of the first houses built in Frankfort. John Instone constructed a cabin here before 1786. He was a boat-builder for General James Wilkinson, the founder of Frankfort. Instone named the street Wapping for a familiar section in London, England. His wife was Ann Elizabeth Benares, the daughter of the Governor-General of the West Indies. His mother, accustomed to society of the French court, no longer captivated with Frankfort, moved to New York where the family had been associated with John Jacob Astor. In 1799 Instone purchased 300 acres on Benson Creek where he located his slaves. He developed a rope and bagging factory, and a line of boats that brought merchandise from Louisville to the river towns and to the interior by wagon. John Bibb bought the house and erected this present Gothic Revival home. Much of the original lumber from the Instone home was utilized in the construction of Gray Gables.

The house has twenty-one rooms, five of which servants utilized. Nearly all the rooms have original floors. Sources say the ironwork on the front is from Birmingham, England. At one time Gray Gables was the home of the Kentucky Commissioner of Fish and Wildlife, Minor Clark. He thought so much of the home that there is reference to it on his tombstone where he is buried in the Frankfort Cemetery.

Today attorney William M. Johnson owns this historic house. His grandfather, L. F. Johnson, has written extensively on Frankfort and Franklin County. His *History of Franklin County, History of Franklin County Bar, Famous Kentucky Tragedies and Trials,* and *History of the Frankfort Cemetery*, provide a rich and thorough legacy of local research.

John Bibb developed the popular Bibb Lettuce in the rear of this home.

Graham Vreeland House CIRCA 1913 — VAUXHALL (GARDEN HALL) 417 WAPPING STREET

Graham Vreeland, founder, editor, and publisher of the Frankfort *State Journal*, built this elegant Georgian mansion in 1913. The architect was D.X. Murphy famed for building the grandstand with its twin spires at Churchill Downs in Louisville. There were fountains, a garden, a pergola, a teahouse and even a garage with a gasoline pump. Inside, the floors, doors and woodwork were solid mahogany. There was a bell-call system and built-in vacuum and sprinkler systems. The floors contained a layer of cinders for resilience. The entire framework was of poured concrete and brick, with floors and walls eighteen inches thick. The basement had five large rooms and bath. One room included a large door, completely barred, for storage of valuables. The four bathrooms, kitchen and garage were lined with white glazed tile. All light fixtures in the baths were of German silver and the hardware of fine brass. It is ironic that such an illustrious house is located on the site of "the White Row," a group of cottages not famed for respectability. The Frankfort City Directory of 1910 lists Frankfort's legendary painter Paul Sawyier as residing in one of the cottages.

Graham Vreeland House

Graham Vreeland started the State Journal in 1912, still serving as Frankfort's newspaper today. (2002)

Mr. Vreeland never aspired for public office, but three years after his sudden death, his widow Anne served on the city council. As a legislative reporter, political writer and managing editor for the Louisville *Courier Journal*, as well as publisher of the Frankfort *State Journal*, Vreeland's influence was widely felt throughout the state.

In October of 1908, Graham Vreeland began the *Frankfort News*, which remained in circulation until 1911, when it merged with the *Kentucky Journal*. This merged paper became the *Frankfort News-Journal*. The paper, re-named *The State Journal* in June of 1912, became one of the most politically influential papers in the state of Kentucky.

Graham Vreeland died July 15, 1920, and was buried with his wife, Anne, in the Frankfort Cemetery.

South-Willis House CIRCA 1875 — 505 WAPPING STREET

This home has connections to three Republican governors. John Glover South was married to Christine Bradley, the only daughter of Kentucky's first Republican governor, William O'Connell Bradley, inaugurated in December of 1895. Governor Bradley's sister, Catherine, would become the mother of Governor Edwin Porch Morrow, elected in 1920. Morrow would die in this home of a heart attack while visiting on June 15, 1935. Former governor Simeon Willis lived here in the mid-1960s.

John G. South served as Minister Plenipotentiary of the United States to the Republic of Panama, appointed by Republican President Warren G. Harding, and to the Republic of Portugal for three years.

South was born in Frankfort on January 23, 1873. Colonel Samuel South, his father, received the Confederate Medal of Honor for gallantry at Chickamauga. The Confederate government only awarded forty such medals. John was the great-grandson of Major John South, an officer during the Revolutionary War. His grandfather was among the first to arrive at the Solomon P. Sharp house following his assassination in 1825. His sister, Mary Ellen, was the mother of the distinguished Major General Edgar Erskine Hume, United States Army Medical Corps, and the most decorated medical general in the history of U.S. combat. Hume is buried in Arlington National Cemetery.

Simeon Willis was residing here at the time of his death on April 2, 1965. Before becoming governor, he was an attorney who served on the Kentucky Court of Appeals. He was governor from 1943 to 1947. His wife, Ida Lee Willis, was instrumental in preserving much of downtown Frankfort's historic district. Their daughter, Sarah Lesly, married Judge Henry Meigs and for a time, lived in the Graham Vreeland mansion a few doors nearby at 417 Wapping Street.

Governor Willis was born in Lawrence County, Ohio, on December 1, 1879. His family moved to Greenup County, Kentucky, when he was ten years old. He became a schoolteacher and served as principal of a three-room grade school in what is now South Portsmouth, Ohio. Following his term as Governor, he was on the Public Service Commission and the state Parole Board. He and his wife are buried in the Frankfort Cemetery.

Pruett House CIRCA 1928 — 511 WAPPING STREET

This home was built for Juanita Kline, granddaughter of Woodford County cattleman and distiller, Col. E.H. Taylor, Jr., and her husband, John William Pruett, a long-time cashier at the old National Branch Bank of Kentucky. Their children, Miss Rebecca K. Pruett and John William (Bill) Pruett, Jr., lived here. Rebecca Pruett authored an informative booklet, *The Browns of Liberty Hall*, in 1966 for the National Society of the Colonial Dames of America in the Commonwealth of Kentucky.

The first floor consists of a beautiful open entry hall running for almost the entire depth of the house. On one side is a large living room with fireplace adjacent to a screened in porch overlooking the Kentucky River. There are four bedrooms on the second floor plus a sunroom. The floors are oak throughout with crown molding.

The Pruetts, a long-time Franklin County family, are buried in the Frankfort Cemetery. Rebecca and Bill's grandfather was John W. Pruett, a Frankfort printer and clothing dealer and Master Mason with Hiram Lodge #4 F and AM.

Chapter Two
WILKINSON STREET

Wilkinson Street, named on behalf of Frankfort's founder, General James Wilkinson, began at the Kentucky River's edge and ran in a northerly direction toward Leestown, a mile above Frankfort. Wilkinson established a ferry at its southern most end as part of his agreement with Virginia to constitute the town.

When Wilkinson developed the town, he was Commander-in-Chief of the Western Division of the United States Army. Born in 1757 in Maryland, he went to Philadelphia for his higher education, became involved with the American Revolution, and embarked upon an illustrious career with George Washington, Benedict Arnold, Horatio Gates, Arthur St. Clair and Aaron Burr, participating in battles at Quebec, Trenton, Princeton, Ticonderoga and negotiating Burgoyne's surrender at Saratoga.

Wilkinson settled in Kentucky around 1783, founded Frankfort in 1786 and was instrumental in the conventions leading to Kentucky's statehood. Under his military leadership, Wilkinson assisted the settlers in their struggle against the Indians in Kentucky and Ohio. In 1805, at Aaron Burr's request, President Thomas Jefferson appointed Wilkinson Governor of the upper Louisiana Territory with headquarters in St. Louis.

In 1811 Wilkinson became part of the Spanish Conspiracy with Aaron Burr and was court-martialed on charges of treason, but acquitted. In later times evidence was uncovered that would have called for his conviction. Following his discharge from the U. S. Army, he made considerable investments in Mexico and died there in 1825. He was buried in Mexico City.

When Wilkinson established Frankfort he reclaimed the lower portions of the town from its swampy condition. The Kentucky River often spilled over into the area that became Frankfort, creating a mosquito-infested, marshy, uninhabitable environment. He had this section ditched and drained laying out the streets of what would become Kentucky's capital city.

Frank W. Sower House

Mr. Sower was the first recipient of the Frank Sower Tourism Award, named in his honor.

Frank W. Sower House
CIRCA 1910 — 112 WILKINSON STREET

Former Frankfort Mayor Frank W. Sower was born in this house built by his father John R Sower in 1910. The Sower family has a long tradition of service to its community. Peter Christian Sower was a member of the Frankfort city council, and his son, the late John R. Sower served on the council and acted as mayor pro-tem. Frank W. Sower was mayor of Frankfort from 1968 to 1972. His son, John Sower II, served as city commissioner before later holding the city's mayoral position from 1980 to 1984.

Arriving here shortly after the Civil War, Peter Christian Sower opened a bakery in 1871. Around 1890, the Sowers opened a hardware store on Main Street and two years later moved to the St. Clair Street location now housing Sower Office Equipment across from the courthouse. Frank Sower turned the business over to his son John in 1986. Frank's father, John, purchased a field for the city when the school's football program was in danger of elimination in the 1920s. Sower Field is located in Bellepoint. The field is still in use for city high school and middle school football and soccer games. Several other Frankfort athletic sites bear the Sower family name.

Throughout his life, Frank Sower has been involved in civic, educational, and charitable affairs. Aside from serving as mayor of the city, he is a past-president of the Kentucky Historical Society, and the charter president of the local Chamber of Commerce. His love and devotion for his community developed his interest in Frankfort history. In 1994 he published his *Reflections on Frankfort 1751-1900*, an account of Frankfort's colorful past featuring a special section on historic North Frankfort where he conducted popular walking tours. He was the first recipient of the Frank Sower Tourism Award, named in his honor, for outstanding commitment of time and effort to tourism in the Frankfort area.

It is no wonder he is so closely associated with history, he seems to have been destined to it. At Frank Sower's birth on December 10, 1910, he was baptized by one of John Hunt Morgan's former Confederate raiders, Rev. Thomas Major. The Sower home is adjacent to the corner site of the famous two-story log house built by Frankfort founder James Wilkinson in 1786. The Kentucky Legislature held assembly in the log house during the early days of statehood. The log house was where former Vice President Aaron Burr stayed while undergoing his first treason trial and his successful defense by Henry Clay. France's Prince Louis Philippe and the Marquis de Lafayette also visited there. Not far from Thomas Major's gravesite in the Frankfort cemetery are the graves of Mr. Sower's father and grandfather.

Orlando Brown House CIRCA 1835 — 218 WILKINSON STREET

Orlando Brown was the second son of Kentucky's first senator, John Brown of Liberty Hall. Born in Frankfort in 1801, Orlando built a career in journalism. He was owner and editor of the *Frankfort Commonwealth* in 1833, and appointed Kentucky's Secretary of State by his friend, Governor John J. Crittenden in 1848. He served as Commissioner of Indian Affairs under President Zachary Taylor. One account says that Orlando has the distinction of being the first honorary Kentucky Colonel. He also served as the Kentucky Historical Society's first corresponding secretary at its founding in 1836.

Distinguished architect Gideon Shryock, builder of Frankfort's Old Capitol and the Franklin County courthouse, designed this structure in 1835. This appears to be the only residence attributed to Shyrock. As was done at Liberty Hall next

door, the brick was fashioned from clay on the property. The front design of the house came from the plan of a country home in England. The style represents a change from Federal to Greek Revival. The floor plan is similar to that in Liberty Hall, but in reverse. Orlando wrote to his wife that he expected the house to cost around five thousand dollars. Today the house contains original furniture, silver, china and brass as well as works by noted artists Matthew Jouett, Robert Burns Wilson, and Paul Sawyier.

As to his talents as a journalist, Washington Irving stated that Brown could have produced works of long-lived literary merit but for his editorial tasks. He died at his home in Frankfort in 1867 and is now resting in the Frankfort cemetery with his family.

In 1955 the daughters of Orlando Brown Jr., Miss Anne Hord Brown and Miss Mary Watts Brown, bequeathed the property to the National Society of the Colonial Dames of America in The Commonwealth of Kentucky. It is maintained as a museum house in conjunction with Liberty Hall Historic Site.

Liberty Hall

Liberty Hall CIRCA 1796 — 218 WILKINSON STREET

Born in Staunton, Virginia, John Brown was the first member of the Congress of the United States from west of the Allegheny Mountains. When Kentucky attained statehood in 1792, Brown became one of the Commonwealth's first senators. He counted among his close friends George Washington, John Adams, Thomas Jefferson, James Madison, James Monroe and George Rogers Clark. Though extensive research has not verified it, many sources report that while in the Revolutionary War he served as an aide to Lafayette and crossed the Delaware River with General George Washington.

On January 18, 1796, John Brown purchased from Andrew Holmes an entire square block in Frankfort bounded by Montgomery (Main) Street, Wapping Street, Wilkinson Street and the Kentucky River. Senator Brown immediately began to construct his home naming it for "Liberty Hall" in Lexington, Virginia, an academy founded by his father and named for their ancestral home in Ireland. Today that academy is Washington and Lee University. It was here at the gardens of Liberty Hall that his wife Margaretta Mason Brown and her friend Elizabeth Love conducted the first recorded Sunday school west of the Allegheny Mountains in 1810.

Liberty Hall became a National Historic Landmark in 1972. The mansion is a wonderful example of Georgian architecture built of brick laid in Flemish bond. The floors throughout are ash. A wide central hall opens on either side into spacious high-ceilinged rooms heated by large fireplaces. The woodwork is black walnut, and the roof and windowsills are cypress. A blacksmith made the few nails used, and the brick for the house was taken from the clay at the foot of the garden extending to the river. In describing the house, the Kentucky Historical Society's Bayless Hardin wrote the following in the April, 1942 Filson Club Quarterly:

"…The wood…was dried for two years under a huge shed. The beams of the lower hall are each a tree that extends its length. Windows are of the twelve paned variety, the glass for which was brought from Philadelphia by mule-back over the Allegheny Mountains, thence by boat to Frankfort The brass locks on the doors came from England. The portal is of noble lines, and above it the most handsome Palladian window to be seen in Kentucky."

Many distinguished guests have been entertained at Liberty Hall, including President James Monroe, Zachary Taylor, Andrew Jackson, Aaron Burr, General Lafayette, Frankfort's founder General James Wilkinson, and Kentucky's great statesman, Henry Clay.

Frankfort will be forever indebted to John Brown, not only for his contributions toward Kentucky's statehood, but to his magnetic persona that caused other influential citizens to settle here.

The National Society of The Colonial Dames of America in The Commonwealth of Kentucky owns Liberty Hall Historic Site. When visiting this landmark be sure to inquire about the "ghost" of Liberty Hall. A photograph exists purported to be "The Grey Lady," Mrs.Brown`s aunt, who died while visiting the residence shortly after arriving from New York. When the Browns died in the late 1830s, they were buried in an early Frankfort graveyard and were re-interred in the Frankfort Cemetery when it opened in the mid-1840s.

Crittenden-Garrard House CIRCA 1795 — 302 WILKINSON STREET

There are few houses in Kentucky like this one built by Jacob Castleman in the mid-1790s. The inner walls are constructed of brick with wood or plaster veneer, a practice common at one time in Boston, Massachusetts. The three-story frame structure features a series of wooden posts filled in with brick and mortar and covered with clapboard. The floors are white ash. All interior doors are of solid, ornately carved yellow poplar, mounted on three brass hinges. During renovation in the late 1970s, a section of an interior wall was glassed-in to show the unusual brick and timber construction. Architect William Gray believes the clapboard to be original. Modernization of the mantels took place during the Victorian era. The three separate rooms on the third floor may have been servant's quarters.

Although the Kentucky Historical Society's Bayless Hardin says a George Adams built the house, most accounts name Frankfort businessman Jacob Swigert as the original owner. Other owners include Dr. Charles C. Pythian, John Harris Hanna, Thomas L. Crittenden, James H. Garrard, Judge J. J. Marshall, W. H. Hoge, John Noonan, and the Commonwealth of Kentucky.

Thomas Leonidas Crittenden was the son of Governor John J. Crittenden, a former U.S. Senator, U.S. Attorney General and close friend of Henry Clay. As a young man Thomas tried his hand at business and failed. He then turned to law, beginning practice in 1843, and was elected Franklin County commonwealth's attorney. During the Mexican War he served on General Zachary Taylor's staff. At the battle of Buena Vista, he was highly distinguished for his gallantry. Through his father's friendship with President Taylor, he received the position of Consulate in Liverpool, England. He fought on the side of the Union during the Civil War, while his brother George sided with the South. Both attained the rank of major general. Crittenden served with distinction at Shiloh, Stones River, and Chickamauga. One of his subordinates described him as tall, slender, with a full black beard and hair down to his shoulders. J.J.Crittenden III, his only son, died with George Armstrong Custer at the Little Big Horn. Thomas and his wife Kitty are buried in the Frankfort Cemetery.

James Henry Garrard, grandson of Kentucky's second governor James Garrard, was a member of the state legislature in 1836. He served as state treasurer for four terms and in 1865 was elected to his fifth term just twelve days before his death. His son, Captain Daniel Garrard, of the 22nd Kentucky Volunteer infantry, died from a head wound during Grant's assault on Vicksburg. Several members of the Garrard family are buried in the Frankfort Cemetery.

Thomas L. Crittenden's son died with Custer at the Little Bighorn.

Dryden-Todd-Starling House CIRCA 1800 — 304 WILKINSON STREET

According to 1810 data, this house was a cabinet-maker's shop. By 1824 it was made into a residence. It is solid brick, with poplar logs set in sand and still contains the original flooring. At first it was only one story, consisting of the present living room and dining room. The windows are Georgian in design and proportion. The upper story was added around 1840. The yellow poplar tree in the front yard predates the town of Frankfort. The tree is over 250 years old.

The yellow poplar tree in the front yard is over 250 years old.

For years this house has been erroneously referred to as "Hallet Hall." Perhaps that name became associated with the house when one of the more recent residents, Harold Collins, wrote a children's book that mentioned a pretended "Hallet Hall." While there have been many prominent residents in this house, none bore the name of "Hallet."

The earliest known owner was carpenter and builder James Dryden. His son, John B. Dryden, was a Federal commissary sergeant in Company E, Ninth Kentucky Volunteers in the Civil War. He advocated community improvements in a paper he published, the *Sunday Call.* For a time he was the lessee and manager of the old opera house, Major Hall, on Main Street, before its destruction by fire in November of 1882. Among those that "trod the boards" were Madam Modjeska, Maurice Barrymore, George Arliss, Lily Langtry, Louisville's Mary Anderson, Buffalo Bill, Wild Bill Hickcock, the Boston Philharmonic, and Blind Tom, the pianist.

Mary Willis Rennick Todd lived here with her children in the 1850s. She was born at historic Glen Willis, built by her grandfather, a short distance north on Wilkinson Boulevard. She married Thomas J. Todd in 1838 and they had six children. Following her husband's death in 1853, in order to provide for her children, the widow Todd taught school. One of those children was her son, Lewis Franklin Todd

During the Civil War, Frankfort soldier Lieutenant L. Frank Todd, 15th Ky. U. S. Infantry, lost his right arm in the battle of Perryville, Kentucky. The Confederates captured Todd and later paroled him. A few months later, a shell at Stones River in Tennessee crushed the back of his head while he attempted to rescue his Rebel-surrounded captain. The enemy stripped him of his clothing and left him for dead on the field. In the same battle, another Frankfort boy died defending the colors for Jefferson Davis. When Private R. K. Woodson, Jr., of the Second Kentucky Regiment saw three of his fellow color bearers successively killed, he picked up the flag, and bearing it in advance of his comrades, gave his life for the Southern cause. He was awarded special recognition for his gallantry by the Confederate government. Today these local soldiers are at rest in the Frankfort Cemetery. Following the war, the widow Todd would marry Woodson's father, Richard Kidder Woodson, settling on a Franklin County farm at Big Eddy on the Kentucky River.

A stray cannon ball struck this house fired from Fort Hill during the attempted Confederate take-over in 1864, leaving a small depression above the front door. Had that skirmish proved successful for Morgan's raiders, it is quite possible they would have sacked the courthouse, burned the Capitol, and destroyed the arsenal, resulting in the capital being moved to another city. Frankfort was the only Union state capitol to be captured by Confederate forces during the Civil War.

Other community leaders and businessmen who lived here include Col. Lyne Starling, Col. E.H.Taylor, Capt.W.T.Gaines, and Fred Sutterlin.

Glen Willis* CIRCA 1815 400 WILKINSON BOULEVARD

Glen Willis was built by Willis Atwell Lee, Jr. in 1815, on a tract of land given to him by his uncle Hancock Lee, the founder of Franklin County's first settlement: Leestown. The house originally faced the Kentucky River. Lee's granddaughter, Mary Willis Woodson, in her recollections, wrote in 1896: "…it was a story and a half high; four rooms and a wide hall on the first floor, and three rooms on the second floor." It contains wide ash floors, finely carved mantels and interior woodwork. Lee served as Clerk of the Kentucky State Senate and was for many years Clerk of the Franklin County and Circuit

Courts. He was a presidential elector for Kentucky in 1817 and again in 1821. When Lee died of typhus in 1824, the property passed to Humphrey Marshall until his death in 1841.

Humphrey Marshall is best known for his *History of Kentucky* (1812), the first real history of the state. Through his marriage to his cousin, he became the brother-in-law of Chief Justice of the United States, John Marshall. As a surveyor, lawyer, and land speculator, he amassed a large fortune. After serving in the Kentucky legislature in 1793 and 1794, he became U.S. senator (1795-1801). He represented Franklin County in the state legislature in 1807, 1808, 1809 and 1823.

It was during the 1808-09 legislative session in Frankfort that the celebrated duel between Humphrey Marshall and Henry Clay took place. The politicians were at odds with each other over the Spanish Conspiracy involving former Vice-President Aaron Burr and Frankfort founder James Wilkinson. Only one seat separated their desks. Clay introduced his so-called homespun resolution encouraging all members of the Kentucky legislature to refuse to buy any article of British manufacture and to patronize only the home industries. As found in the Clay papers of 1809, "they would shun the use of cloth or linens of European fabric until the belligerent nations respect the rights of neutrals by repealing their orders and decrees as relates to the United States." After the introduction of the resolution, Clay, usually a dandy dresser, began to wear ostentatiously a suit of Kentucky homespun jeans, while Marshall arrayed himself in a suit of the finest British broadcloth to show his contempt. The actions resulted in a duel that took place in Indiana across the river from Louisville on January 19, 1809. Though the outcome was not fatal to either combatant, Marshall received a small wound above the abdomen while Clay suffered a thigh wound.

Humphrey Marshall died July 3, 1841. Reverend A. F. Dobbs, of the Church of Ascension, performed the funeral service on the grounds of the old home. Marshall was buried in an unmarked grave nearby. Prominent Frankfort merchant and contractor, Henry Harrison Murray, purchased the property, and in 1887, added the second story, a ballroom on the third floor, and a two-story wing on the right. The wing was removed during restoration efforts by the Franklin County Trust for Historic Preservation in the 1970s.

Suggest driving rather than walking to this location.

Humphrey Marshall fought a duel with Henry Clay in 1809.

The Beeches* CIRCA 1818 — 1503 WILKINSON BOULEVARD

Leestown, one mile north of Frankfort, was one of the first pioneer settlements on the north side of the Kentucky River. Hancock Taylor and the McAfee Company surveyed this area in 1773. Among those surveyors was the famed George Rogers Clark. Leestown, settled by 1775, was named for Hancock and Willis Lee. Hancock's brother was Major John Lee, later one of the founders of Versailles. Leestown became a favorite early pioneer site with a natural river crossing created by buffalo. It was a shipping-port for tobacco, hemp, corn and whiskey. By 1783 the Virginia General Assembly erected a tobacco inspection warehouse. This commercial center was once a contender for the state capital. When a ferry was established at the southern end of Wilkinson Street creating an easier river crossing, it became the end for the burgeoning community. For a time, when the distilleries built up along the river in this area, Leestown was known as Taylorton, after owner Col. E. H. Taylor.

In 1818 Harrison Blanton built the "Beeches," so named for the trees surrounding his property. The Georgian colonial structure with Federal overtones was built with brick in Flemish bond. A feature seldom seen in houses of this type is the Federal style doorway containing much of the original fanlight glass. The double door is batten on the inside and paneled on the outside with the original hardware. The dining room and the parlor contain much detail. The woodwork and mantels in both rooms have Greek Revival overtones. The floors throughout the house are the original ash. Many of the doors have original hardware. The graceful staircase has a lovely cherry newel post and balustrade. Local limestone was chosen for the foundation. The building includes six tripartite windows of Palladian inspiration. The original European beeches were destroyed by blight and replaced by American beeches.

Members of the Blanton family assisted in building both the old Capitol and the new Capitol.

Blanton's construction accomplishments are many. He provided Kentucky River limestone for the present Old Capitol building. He built the Hanna house in 1817, Arrowhead on Versailles Road in 1821, the Governor Charles Morehead house on Shelby Street in 1833, and Wheatland in the Jett area around 1821. He was a friend of architect Gideon Shryock and built the Orlando Brown house on Wilkinson Street based on the architect's design in 1835.

Blanton's son, Benjamin Harrison Blanton, was born in Franklin County, and moved to the western part of the United States. He returned to Frankfort during the Civil War and enlisted in the Confederate Army. He fought under General Hood, and was at the siege of Atlanta. Following the war he returned to Frankfort and lived out his life at the Beeches. He became associated with the nearby Stagg Distillery. In the early 1870s the Ku Klux Klan was quite active in Franklin County. The Klan paid a visit to the Beeches looking for a black man. Not finding him, they instead shot two other blacks living on the Blanton property.

Benjamin Harrison Blanton's son, and third owner of the residence, was James Bacon Blanton. He started a concrete and lumber business around 1917. His company was the chief supplier of materials for the building of the new capitol in South Frankfort, mirroring a similar contribution by his grandfather, Harrison, who furnished materials for the Old Capitol on Broadway in 1827.

Harrison, Benjamin and James Blanton repose at peace in the Frankfort Cemetery.

*Suggest driving rather than walking to this location.

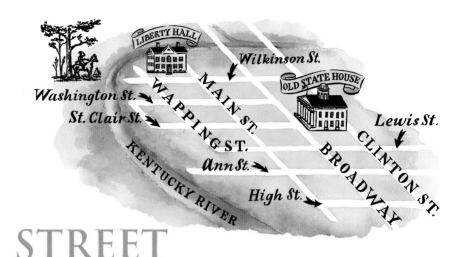

Chapter Three
WASHINGTON STREET

Washington Street, running parallel with Wilkinson Street, was named for General George Washington. Wilkinson was on very intimate terms with the General and served with him during the American Revolution. Washington's chaplain during the Revolutionary War was John Gano, known as "The Fighting Chaplain," who lived in a log cabin across from the Kentucky History Center on Broadway. He was also the Kentucky Legislature's first chaplain. In Gano's burial plot in the Frankfort Cemetery is a marker that says he baptized General Washington.

Letcher-Lindsay House CIRCA 1835 — 200 WASHINGTON STREET

The first building that occupied this corner was a large two-story frame structure erected as a home for Clement Bell. An early pioneer from Salisbury, Maryland, Bell came to Kentucky in 1770 and was the lot's first owner. He and his family lived here for several years until moving beyond the Forks of Elkhorn to his farm "Bell's Grove," off the Georgetown Road. His granddaughter, Jennie Chinn Morton, would later revitalize the Kentucky Historical Society and found its Register. Clement Bell was Justice of the Peace from 1809 to 1816 and served as sheriff of Franklin County.

Thomas Triplett bought the property in 1835, and tore down the frame house and began to build the present home. He died before completing the residence. The next owner was a Dr. Dickinson who finished construction on the house and then shortly died. When Letcher's term as governor expired in 1844, he vacated the High Street gubernatorial mansion and bought this home. In his time, the main entrance, with its portico, was on Wapping Street.

In the late 1870s, the home, originally Greek Revival, underwent a change toward Italianate style. The windows were elongated, openings gained their ornamental hood moldings, and brackets were added to the eaves. Inside, the cast iron mantels date from this period. The building was placed on the National Register of Historic Places in 1971. The house underwent extensive renovation in 1976.

Robert Perkins Letcher, a soldier in the War of 1812, was born in Goochland County, Virginia, in 1788. His parents moved to Garrard County, Kentucky, around 1800. Letcher was a lawyer who served as representative in both the state

legislature and in Congress. He had a winning manner and a pleasant, convivial personality. Successful in thirteen elections, he was a great campaigner with his exhaustible fund of humorous stories, a jug of whiskey to pass around, and his ability to play the fiddle. Letcher, by no means a handsome man, possessed a rotund body, with short arms and legs and a very short neck. He was called "Black Bob" or "Greasy Bob," partly due to his swarthy complexion, but more so because of his wiles as a politician. As governor he proclaimed the first Thanksgiving in Kentucky, twenty years before Lincoln made it a holiday. In 1850, President Taylor appointed him Minister to Mexico for two years. He won all of his political races with the exception of his last, losing a Congressional seat in 1853 to later Vice President John C. Breckinridge. He died at this residence in 1861, and was buried in the Frankfort Cemetery.

On the death of Mrs. Letcher, the house was sold to Judge William Lindsay who was born in Rockbridge County, Virginia. In the 1850s he moved to Clinton County, Kentucky and started a private law practice. During the Civil War he joined the Confederacy, rising to the rank of captain before becoming assistant quartermaster. He served as a staff officer with General Buford and was later on the staff of General Lyons. Paroled as a prisoner of war in 1865, he returned to Clinton County. Lindsay was state senator for one term, judge of the court appeals for eight years, and chief justice for two years when he retired and moved to Frankfort to practice law. He was in the U.S. Senate for several years, practiced law in New York City for a time and served as regent for the Smithsonian Institution.

The Frankfort Woman's Club began in September of 1894. Among their objectives was to have a free library to serve the community. In 1925 they purchased this building for $16,000 and operated the library from this location until the mid-1960s.

First United Methodist Church

CIRCA 1858 — 211 WASHINGTON STREET

In 1790, the first Methodist Conference in Kentucky made Frankfort part of the Lexington circuit. The Frankfort Methodist church began sometime in the early 1820s, largely through the efforts of pastor William Holman. In 1823, Benjamin Hickman donated a lot on Ann Street for the first church building. This small frame structure was in use until 1849, and then replaced with a brick church. Today the site is the John Haly house at 410-412 Ann Street across from the Kentucky History Center. Fire destroyed the brick facility in 1854. While searching for a location to build a new church, the congregation worshipped in the Odd Fellows Hall on Broadway. The membership procured the Harvie Lumber Company and the old celebrated Mansion House Livery Stable at this site on Washington Street. This was also the location of one of Frankfort's first residents Jerry Gullion, who lived in a cabin on this site in the 1780s. Erection of the present Gothic Revival building was in the mid-1850s. A stone front added in 1886 contains a memorial tablet inscribed to honor Jacob Swigert, Sr. for his financial generosity to the church.

The Averill property, adjacent to the church at 207 Washington Street, was built by Marvin Dennison Averill and designed by architects Clarke and Loomis in 1905 using the same plan they used in building the Senator Paynter home on the northeast corner of Shelby and Third Street. The Averill's daughter, Margaret, lived here until the church purchased the property in 1985.

One of the members of the church was Hubbard Hinde Kavanaugh, whose uncle of the same name was a bishop in the Methodist Church. He was born at Mount Sterling, Kentucky in 1836. Following his education, he served as a prescription druggist before becoming a minister in the Methodist Episcopal Church. Arrested during the Civil War on the usual charge of disloyalty, Kavanaugh was released after examination. He joined Morgan's Cavalry and later served as chaplain of the Sixth Kentucky Infantry suffering severe wounds on three occasions. In 1883, Kentucky Governor Luke Pryor Blackburn appointed Kavanaugh chaplain of the Frankfort Penitentiary. He was appreciated as one of the most eloquent and gifted ministers in the state.

Dr. Henry Clay Morrison, who ministered to the church in the latter 1800s, founded and became the first president of Asbury Theological Seminary in Wilmore. During the flood of 1937, the church was used as a depository for clothing that had been collected from across the state by the Red Cross. For two Sundays the congregation worshipped around the corner with their friends at the First Presbyterian Church until the volumes of clothing were distributed.

People in the downtown area have enjoyed inspiring religious melodies since 1978 when the Schulmerich Carillon was installed. In 1985 Don and Toni Wood donated the adjacent historic Todd house, fronting on Wapping Street, to the church. For detailed information on the 1812 Todd house, refer to the Wapping Street chapter.

Macklin House CIRCA 1850 — 212 WASHINGTON STREET

The original building on this site was a single two-story brick house built by a blacksmith named Campbell. John Hart, another blacksmith, bought it, but operated his shop across the street where the Methodist Church now stands. About 1850, a Mr. Drake from Mason County, Kentucky, bought it, tore down the house and built the present home, using the contracting services of Hiram Berry. This is an excellent example of an early American townhouse. At the rear of the building is a lovely two-story brick carriage house built about the same time, one of the few left in Franklin County.

Macklin House

Frankfort's first telephone was installed here in 1878.

The Macklins were extensive landowners in the Forks of Elkhorn area. Alexander W. Macklin owned a large farm, developing a highly lucrative pork slaughtering and packing business. In the 1850s, they averaged slaughtering more than 10,000 hogs a year. The largest number killed in a day was 804. In 1831 he served as constable. In 1843 he built a milldam, still standing, nine feet high across Elkhorn Creek. After his death in 1863, his sons continued to build on their father's fortune, dabbling in horses, whiskey and coal.

George B. Macklin, one of the sons, moved to this location in 1867. He moved to town because he found it hard to keep his servants out in the country due to emancipation following the Civil War. On April 2, 1869, a spectacular blaze swept through his whiskey warehouse near the St. Clair Street Bridge. The warehouse contained 3,500 barrels of whiskey that ignited and drained down onto the Kentucky River surface. Soon the river was afire, casting a bluish flame for some distance. The bridge caught fire several times, but it suffered no actual structural damage. The warehouse was a total loss and cost the insurance companies $350,000.

In 1878, Macklin installed the first telephone in Frankfort. The phone lines ran between his coal company office at St. Clair and Wapping to the coal yard at the end of Broadway by the railroad bridge. The novelty was quite exciting for customers, as Macklin permitted them to phone their orders from his office to the coal yard. The newspaper, *Kentucky Yeoman*, for March 2, that year stated the following: "…we believe its wonderful power, simplicity, and cheapness will soon have a serious effect on the telegraph." He eventually employed four instruments, one at his office, one at the coal yard, one at the scales and another at the apartment of the man in charge of the weighing.

The Macklin family is buried in the Frankfort Cemetery.

Brown-Swigert-Taylor House CIRCA 1815 — 300 WASHINGTON STREET

Dr. Preston W. Brown was the youngest of the eleven children of Reverend John Brown. Preston's brother, John, Kentucky's first U.S. Senator, built Liberty Hall in Frankfort. Another brother, James, was minister to France during President James Monroe's administration and presented the Monroe Doctrine to that country. Still another brother, Samuel, was an eminent physician and professor of medicine at Transylvania University in Lexington. Samuel was a pioneer in cowpox-vaccination against smallpox, introducing it in 1801. In 1815, Preston built the original house on this corner, a four-room dwelling that faced Main Street, on land once owned by Kentucky's third governor Christopher Greenup. When Jacob Swigert became the owner in the 1840s major additions to the house occurred. When viewed from Main Street you can distinguish the original house and its foundation.

Brown-Swigert-Taylor House

Preston was born in Augusta County, Virginia, in that part now incorporated in Rockbridge County. He studied medicine in Staunton, Virginia, and in Philadelphia. In the late 1790s, he moved to Kentucky with his father and settled in Woodford County and later Frankfort, where he developed a large and successful medical practice. He moved his family to Louisville in 1826, where he died at the hands of an assassin. An innocent bystander, he was in the wrong place at the wrong time.

In the 1840s, Jacob Swigert purchased the property and added an attic story, re-orienting the entrance to Washington Street. Jacob and his brother Philip were committed to the growth and development of Frankfort, not just as a matter of economic self-interest, but with heartfelt obligation due to their successes. They were heavily involved in the school system, railroads, banking, local roads, a stagecoach company, a woolen factory, a pork rendering plant, the waterworks, gasworks, hotels, steamboats, the Frankfort Cemetery, and at one time they owned the largest Jersey cattle herd in the United States. They served their community through government leadership as well. Philip was sheriff of Franklin County, Circuit Court Clerk, state senator, and Frankfort's mayor for twenty years. Jacob served as Clerk of the Kentucky Court of Appeals and Franklin County judge.

Colonel Edmond Haynes Taylor, Jr. lived in this house in the early 1870s. L.F. Johnson, in his *History of Franklin County*, called Taylor the "veteran war horse of local politics." He served as Frankfort mayor for over ten years, and two terms each as state representative and state senator. He was the grandnephew of President Zachary Taylor. He proved to be a genius in the merchandising, financing and promotion of liquor. In 1868 he established three modern distillery complexes in the Frankfort area: Old Taylor, the castle-like plant at Millville; Carlisle and O.F.C. (Old Fire Copper) at Leestown; and The Hermitage on the Kentucky River between Second and Fourth Streets. At age 84, he started a successful Hereford stock farm in Woodford County and astonished his friends by paying more for a bull to lead the herd than had ever been paid before. He was instrumental in beginning a railroad line between Frankfort and the Big Sandy River in eastern Kentucky to keep the price of coal down. The Colonel was reputedly the best-dressed man throughout the South. Tailors in New York and Chicago would fit his clothes and he never had less than one hundred suits, which were always in style.

The most famous home associated with Taylor was "Thistleton," a typical Bluegrass estate of 1,000 acres. It was located across from Juniper Hill City Park on Louisville Road. He even had a well-stocked lake on the grounds where his guests could catch their own fish for breakfast. His library contained black walnut bookcases reaching from the ceiling to the floor.

Colonel E. H Taylor is buried in the Frankfort Cemetery.

Swigert-Milam House CIRCA 1835 — 308 WASHINGTON STREET

This Greek Revival home with Gothic overtones, built in 1835 by Jacob Swigert, served as an office while he was clerk of the Kentucky Court of Appeals. At first, the house had only the two front rooms. The basement cellar walls are large stones from the nearby Kentucky River. Expansion of the house occurred during the middle 1860s. It would later become the home of John Milam, who inherited his father's famous fishing reel manufacturing company in the early 1900s. Milam added the beautiful wrap-around Adam mantle found in the right front room. The house would remain in the family until 1969.

One of the first known fishing-reel makers was George Snyder, who operated a shop in Paris, Kentucky around 1810. He was actually a watchmaker but made a few reels for his own amusement. Twenty years later, another watchmaker, Theodore Noel, made some reels at his shop in Frankfort. He probably patterned his reel-making ideas from studying the work of Snyder.

In 1835 Jonathan Meek was a watchmaker in business at 222 West Main Street, Frankfort. His eighteen-year-old younger brother Benjamin worked for him as an apprentice. Benjamin always desired to make a more modern fishing reel. The jewelry store was on the first floor and the reel shop would operate on the second floor. John Milam's father, Benjamin C., became an apprentice with the Meeks when he was sixteen.

Mason Brown, son of John Brown of Liberty Hall, was a noted angler. While visiting with the Meeks at their shop,

he mentioned he could enjoy his fishing more if he had a better reel. That was all the encouragement Benjamin Meek needed. From that discussion came their world famous fishing reel company. Jonathan continued working in the watch-making business, while his brother and Milam moved upstairs and began manufacturing reels.

An Englishman, passing through Frankfort, purchased a reel and returned with it to England. This started a flood of orders from Britain. Shortly the news of the invention spread around the world. In 1839, the brothers formed a partnership under the name J. F. and B. F. Meek. Benjamin Cave Milam worked for the Meeks during this period joining the partnership in 1848. The firm folded in 1852 and Jonathan moved to Louisville where he continued in business as a jeweler-watchmaker until his death. On January 1, 1853, Benjamin Meek became partners with Benjamin Milam in the old Frankfort location. Meek did the jewelry work while Milam made the reels, stamping them "Meek & Milam." This firm dissolved in 1855 with Meek taking over the jewelry store side of the business and Milam operating the fishing-reel manufacturing. Milam realized the value of the name Meek on a reel, so he

Swigert-Milam House

continued to stamp them "Meek & Milam" for twenty-five years. Ben Milam continued to make his own reels at 222 West Main until he died at the age of eighty-three in 1904. His son, John, would carry on the business until 1927. The Milam reels won medals at the International Fisheries Exposition in Bergan, Norway, the Columbian Exposition in Chicago, the International Exposition at Paris, and the Louisiana Purchase Exposition in St. Louis. In 1991, collectors paid $45,000 for four of the antique reels in Kennebunkport, Maine. Even Presidents William McKinley and Teddy Roosevelt were proud possessors of the famous reels. The popular reels are on display at the Kentucky History Center and the Kentucky River Authority Museum at 407 West Broadway.

During the Mexican War, Ben Milam was twenty-five years old when he commanded Company C, of the 1st Kentucky Mounted Volunteer Regiment, joining General Zachary Taylor, commander of the U.S. Army in Mexico.

The families of both the Meeks and the Milams rest today in the Frankfort Cemetery

Ascension Episcopal Church CIRCA 1850 — 311 WASHINGTON STREET

In 1836 the Frankfort Episcopal Church began in John Pendleton's small law office. It was located at the rear of John Harvie's home, today known as the Morehead house at the northeast corner of Main and Washington Streets. With a down payment of $1,000, a gift (or some say a loan) from the Church of Ascension in Greenwich Village, New York, John Woods constructed a small frame Greek Revival church. To show their gratitude for the New York gift, the Frankfort church was named Church of the Ascension. For $500, the first known organ in Frankfort was purchased from John Goodman's piano company on Main Street.

One of the most influential rectors of the early church was John Nicholas Norton, who served for twenty-four years, arriving in 1846. Under his guidance the church grew at a phenomenal rate. He established free schools for the poor, one for the boys, St. John's, and one for the girls, St. Mary's. He founded churches in Versailles and Georgetown. Norton led services at the local penitentiary, at Bridgeport and in Lawrenceburg. Following the Civil War he assisted in starting a school for African-American children that developed into the First Corinthian Baptist Church. In 1849 the Diocesan Convention was held in Frankfort and among the delegates was Henry Clay. In 1853, former President Millard Fillmore attended a Thanksgiving service here. Norton started an orphan's home for girls (still standing at 109-113 West Third Street) in 1860. Norton and his family lived in the Morehead house at 217 Shelby Street.

During Norton's ministry, John Harris Hanna donated $20,000 to construct the present Gothic Revival church. The Hannas arranged for Indiana architect Matthew Temperley to design the church similar to one John had seen in England. The laying of the cornerstone was on August 8, 1850 with the building completed on August 12, 1852. In 1868 an apse and transept were added and by 1899 a new chapel and parish were annexed. The older church remained in use as classrooms for Bible school classes on Sunday and as an educational center for underprivileged children during the rest of the week. In 1870 Norton and his family moved to Louisville. When Norton died, his wife donated their Jefferson County property to establish the famous Norton Infirmary, named for her husband.

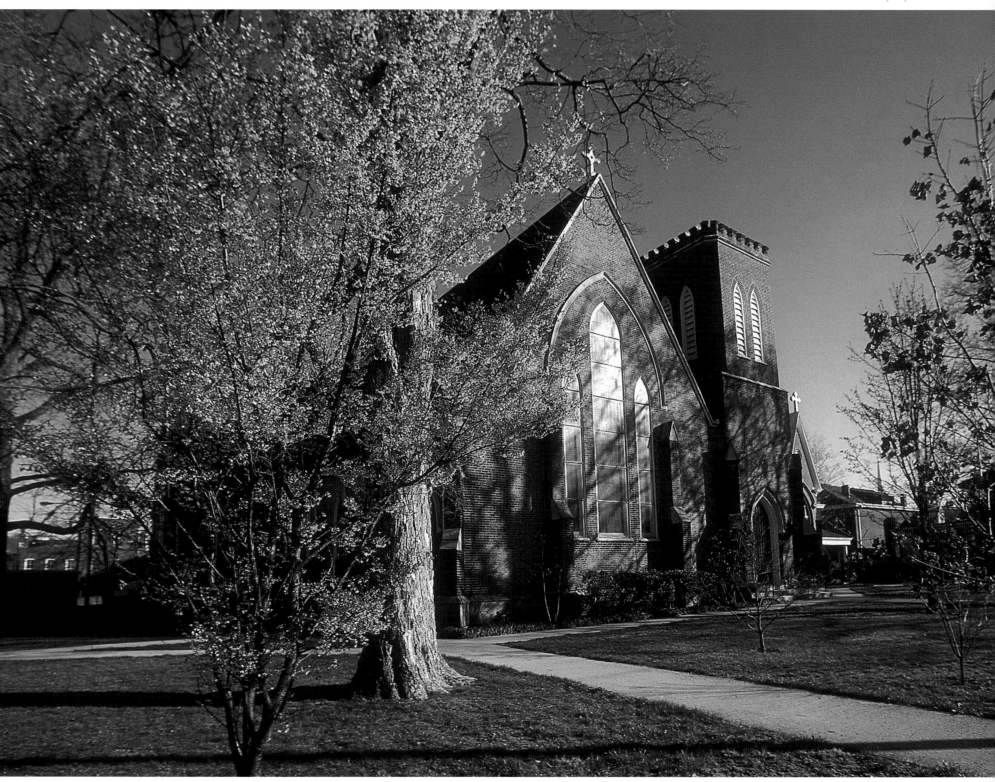

Ascension Episcopal Church

Rev. Charles Clifton Penick served four years as rector of the church, retiring upon the death of his wife in 1912. He enlisted in the Confederate Army on June 9, 1861 and served with George E. Pickett, the leader of the famous charge at Gettysburg.

The primary financial assistance to the church was provided by John Harris Hanna and his wife, Mary, daughter of John Hunt, reputed to be Kentucky's first millionaire. The Hunt-Morgan house in Lexington was the home of Mary's father and also her nephew, General John Hunt Morgan. Hanna, from Pennsylvania, arrived in Kentucky in 1811. He was an attorney, and served as Clerk of the U. S. Circuit and District Courts for thirty years. When the Farmers Bank opened in 1850, Hanna was its first president.

Historian Charles Hinds has provided an exceptional account on the Hanna family in his 1996 book *Ascension Episcopal Church*. The Hannas only had two children, both dying in infancy. Upon the deaths of Mrs. Hanna's sister and her husband, they adopted their two children, John Wesley Hunt Reynolds and Catherine Grosh Reynolds. Catherine would marry and move away. J. W. became a well-known equestrian and wealthy real estate dealer. His daughter, Christine Hunt Reynolds, ran the Fleetwood Horse Farm and Dairy located near the Capital City Airport on Louisville Road. She never married but did adopt a little girl, Marietta Jackson, who when grown, married Miss Reynold's farm manager, George Shanklin Boswell, Jr.

A devastating fire occurred at the church on All Saints Day, Sunday, November 1, 1896. It is ironic that the sermon text for that morning was " Who maketh his angels spirits; his ministers a flame of fire," Psalms 104:4. Parishioners used the old Greek Revival church, later torn down to make way for a residence in 1900, for worship until renovations were completed. The refurbished church opened February 14, 1897.

The Old Bishop's House adjacent to the church was replaced with a new chapel designed by prominent architect Leo L. Oberwarth and dedicated November 19, 1899. During a severe storm on March 31, 1939, lightning destroyed the church steeple. The insurance money totaled $1,697.72, not enough to replace the wooden spire. The money was used to install a new floor for the church, the old one having been deemed unsafe because of termites.

The vestry list of those who served until 1900, include many of the leading citizens of early Frankfort. Among them: Michael Barstow, John Harris Hanna, A. Z. Boyer, B. B. Sayre, Daniel W. Lindsey, S. I. M. Major, Grant Green, B. B. Blanton, J. W. H. Reynolds, Orlando Brown, and Fayette Hewitt.

Landon Thomas House CIRCA 1840 — 312 WASHINGTON STREET

  Emily Harvie Thomas was born in Ashland, Virginia on March 21, 1794. A few years after her birth, her parents Edmund and Anne Thomas, moved to Kentucky. In 1798, her father, Edmund Thomas, succeeded Baker Ewing as the second registrar of the Kentucky Land Office. Landon Thomas, Emily's brother, was born the next year, October 31, 1799. Following the end of his term in 1803, Edmund retired with his family to their large frame house adjacent to the present Red Cross building on the corner of Washington and Broadway. When their father died in 1804 Henry Clay, a close friend of the family, became Emily's legal guardian. In 1818, Emily moved to Augusta, Georgia, to live with Colonel Nicholas Ware's family for the winter. That year she met and married Richard Tubman, an Englishman from Maryland. Her husband voiced concern that she might come down with yellow fever and made her promise that she would spend her summers in Frankfort. This she did for the rest of her life. Richard died in 1836, leaving her with a huge estate and a substantial inheritance.

Landon Thomas House

In 1840, Landon Thomas, by now a prosperous attorney, built this brick Federal-style home with Italian influence. It contained a large glassed-in solarium with tile floor. The family used it as a bird sanctuary. In 1872, Landon spent $10,000 on improvements to the house. The home remained in the Thomas family until sold in 1938 to the LeComptes, who made it into a funeral home. The bay extension was added during the LeCompte family's residency. The old carriage house still exists in the rear of the funeral home.

Landon Thomas served on the committee to re-inter the remains of Daniel and Rebecca Boone in the Frankfort Cemetery on September 13, 1845. That day all business in the city was suspended and the entire community, as well as most of the counties in the Commonwealth, were on hand for the ceremonies. In 1847 Thomas was elected to the state legislature in the House of Representatives. That same year he served as Chief Assistant Marshall in the funeral procession burying the bodies of honored Kentuckians, including the son of Henry Clay, who fell at Buena Vista during the Mexican War. Estimated crowds were between 15,000 and 30,000. From the battery stationed in the cemetery, cannon fired every hour from sunrise to ten o'clock. The speaker was John C. Breckinridge. During the 100th anniversary of the founding of Frankfort, Thomas contributed an article to the centennial celebration, October 6, 1886. A crowd estimated at 25,000 was on hand for the largest parade in town up to that time. Landon Thomas died on October 2, 1889, almost three years later to the day.

Henry Clay was an important leader of the American Colonization Society. Clay regarded slavery as evil although he himself owned slaves. The purpose of the society was to promote the colonizing "of the free people of color in the United States, with their own consent, in Africa." Emily Tubman was of the same persuasion. In 1842 she offered 144 American born slaves on her Georgia plantation their freedom. Sixty-nine agreed to re-settle in Liberia. Out of her own pocket she paid the migration cost of over $6,000. A town in Maryland County, Liberia, bore the name of Tubman. William Tubman, the grandson of two of her former slaves, became the eighteenth president of Liberia, serving from 1944 to 1971.

Emily Tubman was quite generous with her fortune. She contributed to the Midway Orphan School, Millersburg College, Kentucky University and endowed a chair at Bethany College. Ms. Tubman expended over $26,000 of her personal fortune to restore the First Christian Church following its destruction by fire in 1870. She passed away June 9, 1885, and is buried with her brother Landon in the Thomas lot in the Frankfort Cemetery.

Foster-McClure House CIRCA 1814 — 318 WASHINGTON STREET

John M. Foster married Governor John Adair's daughter Catherine in Mercer County on February 22, 1814. They lived in this house while he served as registrar of the Kentucky Land Office. Catherine died in 1820 and a year later, Foster married Marcia White. At Foster's death, Landon Thomas, who lived next door, purchased the brick home. In 1857 Agnes Todd McClure and her children moved from Owenton to Frankfort and rented the property from Landon Thomas. Her husband, John Dunn McClure, had died in Owen County the year before. At this time it was a small brick house, built in three parts, with the main entrance facing Broadway. During the Civil War two of her sons, William Thomas and Joseph Lewis, served in the Union's 15th Kentucky Volunteer Infantry. In July 1862 William died of typhoid fever in Huntsville, Alabama. His brother Joseph, wounded at the Battle of Perryville on October 8, 1862, refused to have his leg amputated. Brought home to Frankfort, Joseph died from his wounds a few days later. The brothers were buried side by side in the Frankfort Cemetery. Following the war another younger brother Richard Knott McClure, later a prominent businessman in Frankfort, would purchase the property from the Thomas family. He changed the front of the house to face Washington Street because the passing railroad trains frightened his horses secured out front on Broadway.

Richard K. McClure and his son William founded a successful store in 1870. Located on St. Clair Street they sold shoes, schoolbooks, hats, and stationery. In 1879, McClure started an advertising paper for his store called the *Fireside Journal,* providing information on the best and cheapest boots in town. It was common for shoe stores to sell school supplies. When children would return to school each year, their parents would usually buy them a new pair of shoes. In October of 1897 McClure, and other businessmen and civic leaders, formed the Commercial Club of Frankfort to promote and plan the economic future of the town.

This effort eventually led to the development of the Chamber of Commerce in the early 1900s.

In 1917 the Church of the Ascension bought this property from McClure for $5,975 to use as a rectory. Six years later, the property sold for $8000. Later it would belong to Mrs. Samuel E. Cozine, who ran it as a boarding house. The ten or twelve rooms were easily adapted for this purpose. Today it houses the local chapter of the American Red Cross.

World War I was directly responsible for the organization of the National Red Cross Chapter in Frankfort. Mrs. George Baker and Mrs. Eugene Ray formed the chapter in May 1917. W. Pruett Graham served as the first chairperson and Governor A.O. Stanley was honorary chair. By July headquarters would officially locate in the McClure Building. World War I brought about the most vigorous showing of patriotism since the Civil War. During the months that followed, Red Cross members rolled thousands of feet of bandages and prepared refreshments for soldiers passing through on troop trains heading to the frontlines in Europe.

Chapter Four
MAIN STREET

Main Street, first known as Montgomery Street, was named in honor of British General Richard Montgomery who resigned his commission in 1773 to come to America. When the American Revolution began, he accepted a brigadier general's commission in the Continental Army. In 1775 Montgomery died while leading an unsuccessful attack on Quebec. He was buried without honor in Quebec but Congress ordered his remains removed to New York in 1816 and placed in front of St. Paul's Church, where a monument was erected to his memory. Kentucky's Montgomery County was also named in honor of this soldier.

Labrot-Taylor Home CIRCA 1854 — 421 WEST MAIN STREET

Colonel Orlando Brown built a small house on this site, which became the property of Robert Henry Crittenden, son of Kentucky Governor John J. Crittenden. The original two-room structure with basement was elevated a half story above ground. As the house underwent changes, large basement windows, filled in with grading, brought the present building to ground level.

Robert H. Crittenden, born in 1822, in his early days gave his parents a difficult time. He enrolled in Miami University at Oxford, Ohio, but was lazy and behaved badly. At his father's insistence, Robert returned to Frankfort and attended a local private school, eventually transferring to Centre College in Danville. There he applied himself and graduated under the tutelage of his brother-in-law, and president of the college, Reverend John C. Young. Robert became a prosperous businessman and would make several additions to the house before selling it to Judge Andrew James, Attorney General of Kentucky in 1859. Upon the judge's death, his family sold it to Leopold Labrot who completely changed it. He added the current hall, staircase, living room and front bedrooms.

In 1878, Labrot, a French wine manufacturer, bought half interest in what would become the Labrot & Graham distillery. In the 1790s, Scottish immigrant Elijah Pepper started a distillery in Versailles, located behind the Woodford County courthouse. In 1812, Elijah moved the operation to its present site on the iron-free, calcium-rich waters of Glenn's Creek. Following his death in 1831, his son Oscar was in charge. With the hiring of master distiller Dr. James Crow, inventor of the sour mash process,

Pepper was among the first to begin aging bourbon in charred oak barrels. They called their whiskey "Old Pepper." Among the more famous imbibers were Henry Clay, Andrew Jackson, Daniel Webster, Walt Whitman, and Mark Twain. A new brand, "Old Taylor," was developed when Col. E. H. Taylor bought the distillery from Oscar Pepper's widow and son, James, in the early 1870s. James Graham bought it in 1877. Today Labrot & Graham Distillery is a National Historic Landmark.

Kenner Taylor, a son of the distiller Col. E.H. Taylor, bought the house in the early 1900s adding the front bath, the Federal style porch and the side sun porch. He installed the lovely paneled ceiling in the library and the marvelous mantle.

First Presbyterian Church CIRCA 1849 — 416 WEST MAIN STREET

In 1810 several churches existed in the Franklin county area, but there were no churches located within Frankfort. Margaretta Brown, Senator John Brown's wife, and Elizabeth Love organized the first Sunday school west of the Allegheny Mountains. Classes were either inside Liberty Hall or in the garden outside. The first available church in town occurred when the Kentucky Legislature passed an act granting a $4,000 lottery franchise to build a public place of worship. The structure was located on the southwest corner of the present-day Old Capitol grounds. The Baptists, Presbyterians and Methodists shared services for several years, but friction developed around joint usage and worshiping in a place financed through the means of gambling.

The initial Presbyterian pastor was Eli Smith, born in Massachusetts. He lived at 417 Murray Street and served as a South Frankfort trustee in 1828. It was during his ministry the congregation decided to move from the public worship house. Around 1824 the Presbyterians constructed a brick building at the corner of Wapping and St. Clair. There they held religious services until 1849. That year, they hired Louisville architect and contractor Jacob Beaverson to erect the present building, selling their former location to the Catholic Church. It took many loads of dirt to level the area before construction. When finished, the congregation was justifiably proud of their beautiful modified Gothic Revival brick structure complete with eighty-five foot bell tower. Reverend Stuart Robinson, pastor at this time, would serve until 1853. The first organist of the church was Elizabeth Harlan, the mother of Supreme Court Justice John Marshall Harlan.

Not long after the new building was in use, the church entertained a visit from Zachary Taylor, on his way to Washington for his inauguration. He was in Frankfort trying in vain to persuade Governor John J. Crittenden to serve in his cabinet as Secretary of State. During a three-day fair to raise money for church furnishings, on a platform erected for the occasion, the President-elect sat in an armchair between the Governor and his wife to receive the congregation. Taylor received a Bible from some of the members. Visitors everywhere thronged the beautiful new church on that cold February day in 1849. When former Vice President of the United States Colonel Richard M. Johnson died in Frankfort November 19, 1850, Reverend Robinson provided the funeral message.

Another noted pastor of the church was Beverly Tucker Lacy, serving from 1858 to 1861. Reverend B.T. Lacy was born in 1819, in Prince Edward County, Virginia. In Frankfort, his pro-southern feelings were in conflict with the Northern sympathies of the congregation. He left the church in Frankfort and eventually became Stonewall Jackson's unofficial corps chaplain. He became the personal overseer for the religious needs of ninety-two infantry regiments, twenty-three artillery batteries, and assorted detachments of cavalry. During the war, as a close friend, he often shared living quarters with Jackson, also a staunch Presbyterian. Lacy baptized Jackson's five-month-old daughter, Julia Laura. At Chancellorsville, on May 2, 1863, Stonewall was accidentally shot by his own men, resulting in the amputation of his arm. The task of burying his limb fell to Lacy. When Jackson died May 10, Lacy was nearby in prayer.

Dr. Jesse R. Zeigler began his pastorate at the First Presbyterian Church in 1907. In 1910, while traveling to Europe, he befriended one of the greatest architects of the 20th century, Frank Lloyd Wright. It was on this cruise that Wright designed for Zeigler at 509 Shelby Street, a home that would become the only residence in Kentucky designed by the renowned architect.

First Presbyterian Church

The first Sunday School west of the Allegheny Mountains was started by two members of this church.

Rodman-Bennett-Hazelrigg House CIRCA 1866 — 407 WEST MAIN STREET

Dr. William Barbour Rodman, who built this Victorian home, was a brilliant physician credited with being the first to realize that pneumonia was contagious. He was the oldest brother of Admiral Hugh Rodman who served as Commander of the Pacific Fleet following World War I. His mother, Susan Anne Barbour Rodman, was a descendant of families from Virginia who collectively had ten veterans in the Revolutionary War, nine of whom were commissioned officers of either the army or the navy.

Chief Justice of the Kentucky Court of Appeals Judge Caswell Bennett also lived here. When Bennett died at Hopkinsville in 1894, his body, returned to Frankfort by military escort, lay in state in the statehouse (now the Old Capitol) on Broadway. Public buildings and businesses closed in observance of his death. He is buried in the Frankfort Cemetery.

The property came into the possession of Chief Justice of the Court of Appeals Judge James H. Hazelrigg in 1897. Hazelrigg had served as Montgomery County Judge. He was the first president of the Citizen's Improvement Association in Frankfort, an organization that started in 1909, promoting public playgrounds and kindergartens, conducting sewing classes, starting a sign-removal campaign, and promoting an effort to clean up the riverbank. In 1864 he joined the Confederate army at age 16 and served until the end of the war.

Sometime before 9 p.m. on Wednesday, February 1, 1900, Judge Hazelrigg swore in William Goebel as governor of Kentucky. On January 30, Goebel was shot while walking to the statehouse. He was carried to the office of Dr. H. S. Keller (some accounts say Dr. E.E. Hume) on the corner of Ann and Clinton, examined and removed to his room in the Capital Hotel where the State National Bank is located today on Main Street. The bullet entered Goebel's chest, smashing the sixth rib, forcing bone splinters into his lungs, exiting his back and lodging in a near-by hackberry tree. He contracted uremic poisoning, pneumonia developed, and by February 3, he was dead at age forty-four. Goebel is the only governor in American history to die in office from an assassin's bullet. Again, the services of Judge Hazelrigg were required, this time to swear in Lieutenant Governor J. C. W. Beckham as governor of Kentucky.

Today Rodman, Bennett, Hazelrigg, and Goebel lie at rest in the Frankfort Cemetery.

Judge Hazelrigg swore William Goebel in as governor of Kentucky, the only governor in American history to die in office from the bullet of an assassin.

Crittenden-Watson House CIRCA 1800 — 401 WEST MAIN STREET

John Jordan Crittenden was, perhaps, the greatest man to claim Frankfort as his home. *The Commonwealth*, a Frankfort newspaper, said at his death: "…In all that constitutes true greatness he had no superior. Great without ambition for place or prominence. Patriotic without any selfish inducements, brave, virtuous and self-denying, from the instincts of his nature he was the model of a citizen, a patriot and a gentleman." At his death Kentucky Governor Thomas E. Bramlette proclaimed: " When a great man dies, a Nation mourns. Such an event has occurred…Kentucky's longest tried statesman, a man faithful to every trust, one who has added, by his talents and character, to the fame of the Nation and advanced the glory and honor of his native Kentucky. It is fit and proper that all testimonies of respect and affection should be paid his remains by all in authority as well as by private citizens. I therefore earnestly request that all places of business shall be closed…from the hours of ten o'clock in the morning until five in the afternoon and hereby direct all the public offices in Frankfort to be closed during the entire day." His greatest hour came toward the end of his life, with the beginnings of the Civil War. In early 1861, he sought for a compromise by constitutional amendment and referendum to avert the coming war. The nation's tragedy was demonstrated in his own household as his two sons, each a major general, chose opposite sides in the war.

John Jordan Crittenden was born September 10, 1786, in a log cabin still standing off U.S. 60 a few miles east of Versailles. He attended Kentucky Academy adjacent to Pisgah Presbyterian Church in Woodford County, Washington College (later Washington and Lee) in Virginia, and graduated from Virginia's William and Mary College. He studied with outstanding jurist George M. Bibb, beginning his law practice in nearby Versailles before moving to Russellville in Logan County.

At the age of twenty-two, Crittenden was appointed attorney general of the Illinois Territory. He served in the

Rodman-Bennett-Hazelrigg House

Kentucky House of Representatives in 1811 and would continue for six consecutive terms. During the War of 1812 he was an aide to Governor Isaac Shelby at the Battle of the Thames. The General Assembly selected him to fill a vacancy in the U.S. Senate in 1817. Due to a lack of finances and family responsibilities, he resigned his Senate seat and returned to Kentucky. In 1819 he moved to Frankfort to expand his legal practice. Here he would gain a distinguished reputation as a defense attorney and a politician. Over the years he would serve as legislator, Kentucky's Secretary of State, Governor, United States Attorney General twice and five times as United States Senator. These accomplishments happened while he resided here at the southwest corner of Main and Washington Streets in Frankfort.

Crittenden-Watson House

The two-story Federal style Flemish bond brick building was built on property once owned by Aaron Burr. In the Crittenden biography by Albert D. Kirwan, *The Struggle for the Union*, we read: "It was a spacious, rambling, L-shaped brick house, probably built about the turn of the century and modeled somewhat after the houses of colonial Philadelphia. The front door opened directly on Main Street and was elevated only a step above the street. Inside, a spacious central hall separated the two front parlors, and from this hallway a graceful staircase ascended the left wall to a landing, to halls opening upon sleeping rooms on the upper floors. Behind the house was a small garden, enclosed by a high brick wall. At the front of the house, on the edge of the sidewalk, was a semi-circular carriage block of Kentucky marble." The block was one of two presented to Crittenden. These stones had been part of the doorsteps of one of the former state capitol buildings destroyed by fire. From this stone Crittenden would address his

✦ ✦ ✦ ✦ ✦ ✦ ✦ ✦ ✦ ✦ ✦ ✦ ✦ ✦ ✦ ✦ ✦ ✦

neighbors and constituents on his return trips from Washington.

It was here that Crittenden would entertain his distinguished friends such as Governor Robert P. Letcher and his wife who lived directly behind him on Washington Street; the Orlando Browns and the Mason Browns, who lived around the corner on Wilkinson Street; the Moreheads, who lived diagonally across the street; the Burnleys, Bibbs, and Carneals from Wapping Street. One of Crittenden's best friends, Henry Clay of Lexington, was a frequent visitor. Massachusett Senator Daniel Webster and his family were here in 1837. Vice President of the United States and later Confederate General John C. Breckinridge was here on several occasions. Just before his inauguration, President-elect Zachary Taylor was here to request Crittenden's services in his cabinet in 1848.

Crittenden-Watson House

Crittenden was married three times. His first wife was Sarah O. Lee of Versailles. Among their children was George Bibb Crittenden who fought in the Mexican War and was a major general in the Confederate army. In 1862, as commander in eastern Kentucky at the Battle of Mill Springs, the blame for the collapse of the Confederate right flank fell to him. Following the war he returned to Frankfort and became state librarian from 1867 to 1874. Another child was Thomas Leonidas Crittenden, who was consul to Liverpool, England, and a major general for the Union Army during the Civil War. A daughter, Ann Mary, wrote a biography of her famous father. When Lafayette visited Frankfort in 1825, Ann Mary, age eleven, read aloud to the old dignitary an original poem written for the occasion. Another daughter, Sallie Lee "Maria" Crittenden, was the mother of the U. S. Navy Rear Admiral John Crittenden Watson, who was born in this house. He was on Admiral Farragut's staff during the Civil War and was present at the capture of Mobile Bay. He also commanded part of the Atlantic Fleet during the Spanish American War. Three of the admiral's sons were military officers: a captain in the U.S. Navy, a colonel in the U.S. Army and a major in the United States Marine Corps.

Crittenden's second wife was Maria Knox Todd, daughter of famed Federal Judge Harry Innes. She had been married to her cousin, John Harris Todd, the son of Justice Thomas Todd of the United States Supreme Court. Her husband passed away a few weeks after Crittenden's wife Sarah died. They were married two years later. Maria's daughter, Catherine Todd, would marry her stepbrother Thomas Crittenden. One of their sons, John Jordan Crittenden III, would die with Custer at the Battle of the Little Big Horn.

Crittenden's third wife, Elizabeth Moss, had been married twice before. Her first husband was General Daniel Wilcox and her second, General William Ashley. In the ten years of their life together, Elizabeth would accompany Crittenden on his travels whenever possible. She was with him in Louisville when he collapsed from a probable coronary thrombosis. The next day, Elizabeth accompanied him to Frankfort, to the home in which he had lived over forty years. He died around three o'clock Sunday morning, July 26, 1863. Among his last words were: "Let all the ends thou aimest at be thy country's, thy God's and truth's." Funeral services were held in the First Presbyterian Church across from his home. The church was filled to overflowing and thousands stood in the street outside. General Ambrose Burnside, commander of the Department of Ohio, was among those in the funeral procession that made its way from the church up the Main Street hill to the Frankfort Cemetery. Cannon thundered forth from surrounding hills and reverberations were heard for miles and in the town was heard a continuous tolling of bells from churches all over the city.

George D. Prentice in the Louisville *Journal* wrote, "…More than any other man in the land, Crittenden embodied the spirit and the principle to which…every enlightened American looks for the salvation of the Republic…He was indeed the glass wherein true patriots did dress themselves. But this mirror now lay broken upon the earth, for the true and princely Crittenden is dead."

Charles Slaughter Morehead House CIRCA 1810 — 326 WEST MAIN STREET

Charles Slaughter Morehead was born in Nelson County, Kentucky July 7, 1802. He served in the state legislature as representative, twice speaker of the house, and Attorney General of Kentucky. Following his term as governor, he served in the United States Congress as Representative. Morehead was a member of the committee to superintend the construction of the Franklin County Courthouse completed in 1835. He was related to three governors: James Turner Morehead and Simon Boliver Buckner of Kentucky, and James Motley Morehead, governor of North Carolina. James T. Morehead, Kentucky's first native born governor, also lived in this home for several years.

In the 1830s Morehead and Judge Mason Brown, son of Liberty Hall's John Brown, compiled a new edition of the Laws of Kentucky. Printed in two volumes totaling 1648 pages, the manuscript was entitled *A Digest of the Statute Laws of Kentucky, etc.* Of this work, author Willard Rouse Jillson said "…An altogether scholarly and erudite piece of legal editorial work, the Morehead-Brown compilation of the Kentucky statutes, though succeeded now by numerous more recent and extended works of a similar character, is still found in all good Kentucky law libraries and is often consulted…"

Morehead and his wife, Margaret, loved the arts, reveling in music and theatre. In honor of the support Franklin County gave him during his election, he named one of his sons Franklin. During his term as Kentucky's nineteenth governor, the Kentucky State Agricultural Society received its charter and created the first state fair.

In 1833 Morehead built an impressive home that still stands at 217 Shelby Street in South Frankfort. He sold that property and moved to his Main Street residence in 1847. Following his term, Morehead moved his family to Louisville.

This two-story Flemish bond brick Federal style home of Georgian design was built around 1810. The original owner was Mark Hardin, Registrar of the Kentucky Land office. Prominent Frankfort citizen and legislator John Harvie lived here for

Charles Slaughter Morehead House

While a state legislator, Henry Clay often stayed here during the meetings of the General Assembly.

a time. While Henry Clay served in the state legislature, rather than make the arduous trip back and forth to his Lexington home, he would stay here with Harvie. Alexander Campbell, founder of the Christian Church movement, stayed here on three occasions while John L. Moore resided here. In 1874, railroad magnate Lawrence Tobin purchased the home. The walls of this house are two feet thick. Of special note are the beautiful recessed entrance with sidelights and transom and an attic fanlight window. Inside, a lovely stairway with cherry rail, treads and hand-turned spindles, winds its way to the top floor. Hog-hair and horsehair plasterwork is visible in the attic as well as the basement. Several mantels are original.

In 1861 the Kentucky legislature voted to adhere to the Union. Anyone with leanings toward the Confederacy was in danger of indictment for treason. To Abraham Lincoln, Kentucky was the key to preserving the Union and he would not accept disloyal opposition. Morehead owned valuable property in Tennessee and Alabama, and fostered southern sympathies. Union authorities arrested Morehead at his Louisville residence and, without charge or indictment, sentenced him to prison at Fort Lafayette in New York. He remained imprisoned four months without trial and gained freedom through the intervention of his neighbor and friend, John C. Crittenden. Following the war, he resided at his plantation in Greenville, Mississippi, where he died December 21, 1868. He and his family are buried in the Frankfort Cemetery.

Chapman Coleman Todd House CIRCA 1808 — 333 WEST MAIN STREET

This Federal-style brick structure is built on a stone foundation. A recessed main doorway with leaded fanlight above and rectangular panes on each side is behind an entrance fronted by two flat wooden columns under a narrow overhang. In the late 1800s the front of the house experienced a Gothic "modernization" and the east side of the building was added. Gaslights were installed and the second floor was made into rental apartments. The original mantles and woodwork have been removed but wide ash floors remain. In 1978 the Frankfort Neighborhood Development Agency, assisted by a U.S. Department of Housing and Urban Development grant, selected this house for its pilot program of rehabilitation.

Rear Admiral Chapman Coleman Todd was born April 5, 1848 at this house built by his grandfather John Harris Todd.

Chapman Coleman Todd House

He was the son of Harry Innes Todd, one of the original stockholders of the Farmers Bank, who served as a legislator and twice-elected sheriff from Franklin County. In all probability Chapman got his love for the water from his father who was a riverboat captain. His father commanded the *Blue Wing*, which made a regularly scheduled, twice weekly run between Frankfort and Louisville. Chapman's great-grandfather was Supreme Court Justice Thomas Todd. He was also a step-grandson of political leader John J. Crittenden. During the Civil War there was a need for an increase in the United States Navy and it was Crittenden who arranged for the then thirteen-year-old Chapman to be appointed to Annapolis. He graduated from the naval academy in 1866 and retired in 1902 as Rear Admiral with nearly forty years of service. He was recognized for "eminent and conspicuous conduct in battle" during the Spanish-American War. Commanding the *USS Wilmington*, Todd attacked Cardenas, Cuba in an attempt to capture three Spanish gunboats. He also attacked Manzanilla and burned three Spanish transports. As a midshipman in the United States Navy, Todd received special recognition during the Civil War, was awarded the Spanish Campaign Medal (for service on the *Wilmington*), and was given the Philippine Campaign Medal (for service on the *Brooklyn*). According to local lore Chapman was also the commander of the first exploration up the headwaters of the Orinoco and Amazon Rivers. While it is possible he accomplished the South American adventure following his retirement from the U.S. Navy, there has been no evidence to support this local tradition.

His first wife was Ann Mary Thornton, a sister of the wife of Admiral John Crittenden Watson. His second wife was Eliza James, the mother of Chapman Coleman Todd Jr., who was a lieutenant commander in the United States Navy during World War I. Rear Admiral Todd died in Washington D.C. on April 28, 1929. Chapman and his wife Eliza are buried in the Frankfort cemetery.

Old Farmers Bank Building

Old Farmers Bank Building

CIRCA 1855 — 216 WEST MAIN STREET

The development of Farmers Bank occurred when the Kentucky General Assembly enacted a bill in February of 1850. The first officers and board of directors were a virtual who's who of Frankfort's leading citizens. The first president was businessman and attorney John Harris Hanna who donated the funds to erect the present Church of the Ascension, Mayor Philip Swigert, Secretary of State James Harlan, leading merchant Richard M. Knott, Sr., Woodford County farmer Randolph Railey, and former state auditors John B. Temple and Thomas S. Page. On September 16, 1850 the bank opened on the southeast corner of Main and Lewis Streets. By 1854, needing more space, the bank purchased property across the street jointly owned by Philip Swigert and Captain Isaac Wilson. Builder John Haly, authorized to supervise the construction of the new building, used Kentucky River limestone with gray limestone trimming and raised joints to create the building we have today. The new bank was open for business in 1855. John Haly's relative Dennis renovated the bank interior in 1873. It was the largest bank in Franklin County by the

end of the 1930s. Over the years the bank would outgrow this building and in 1971 a more modern edifice was constructed on the southeast corner of Main and Ann Streets. Today Farmers Bank is the state's second oldest bank (operating on the original charter), and has served as state government's sole depository for almost 80 years.

Noted author and humorist Irvin S. Cobb lived in the top left front corner room while covering the Goebel assassination for a Louisville newspaper in 1900. Paul Sawyier's 1917 painting, *Rainy Day in Frankfort* features this building. Following the Farmers Bank relocation in 1971 the building became the Kentucky Teachers Retirement until 1988.

In 1988 the building became the property of First Federal Bank. While major renovation was required to accommodate First Federal, the style and much of the woodwork, marble, and brass are original. First Federal Savings and Loan Association organized in September 1934 in part because of the Home Owners Loan Act of 1933. Its purpose was to provide a safe, profitable investment opportunity enabling local citizens to save money to buy homes. The bank purchased the old Kagin Brothers Dry Goods building on St. Clair street when they needed more space. They rented part of the building to the Sanitary Laundry and Cusick's Photography Studio. In 1956 they bought the Whitehead and Hancock Plumbing building by the bridge on St. Clair Street. Eventually these buildings were incorporated into a single office complex. The original organizers were J. B. Brislan, Clayton Fincel, Joseph C. Jones, Carl A. Kagin, former Mayor T. E. Kenney, H. K. Rogers, R. S. Scott, Lambert N. Suppinger, and W. P. B. Wachtel.

New Farmer's Bank Building

State National Bank

CIRCA 1923 — 130 WEST MAIN STREET

The corner of Ann and Main Streets is rich in local history. Here stood the famous Weisiger Inn, built by Captain Daniel Weisiger around 1800. Weisiger was Frankfort's first postmaster, serving from October 1, 1794 to July 1, 1795. Following the victorious Battle of the Thames in the War of 1812, a contingent of captured British prisoners-of-war came to Frankfort. The penitentiary housed the enlisted men and the Weisiger House quartered the officers. However, due to public outcry because of the slaughter of Franklin County soldiers earlier at the River Raisin, the British officers were removed to the prison. It was here that Frankfort celebrated with a ball to honor General Lafayette during his 1825 visit to the United States.

In 1850 the old building was replaced with the Capital Hotel. Architect Isaiah Rogers, who built the Galt House in Louisville, designed the building with assistance from Henry Whitestone. The master mason was John Haly. Ex-President Millard Fillmore was entertained here in the mid-1850s. In the late 1850s Tom Thumb came to town with the P.T. Barnum Show and roomed here. He played his concert grand piano, two and a half feet high and three feet long, which is now in the Smithsonian Institute. Tragedy struck here in 1879 when Thomas Buford of Henry County killed Judge John M. Elliott over a court decision. On January 16, 1900, the hotel was the site of a political speech by famed politician William Jennings Bryan. Eighteen shots rang out in the lobby that morning, killing three and wounding three more. A few days later Governor William Goebel died at his room in the hotel following an assassination plot. Fire destroyed the building on April 5, 1917. All that remains is a building section in the rear facing Ann Street. The New Capital Hotel purchased the property in 1921.

The erection of the present building was in 1922 based on a design by Frank L. Packard of Columbus, Ohio, and constructed by Leo L. Oberwarth. The Oberwarth family designed many buildings in Frankfort, including Second Street School, the Frankfort Municipal Building on Second Street and the state police barracks and training center.

In 1964, the building became the home of the State National Bank. The bank received its charter in 1889. The first home of the bank was the Hume Building at the corner of Main and Lewis Streets, across from the old Farmers Bank building. As the bank outgrew its first home, it moved to the northwest corner of Ann and Main in 1912. In the early 1960s, the State Bank would offer Kentucky's first drive-in teller-windows. In the mid 1980s the building underwent a three million dollar renovation. The Whittaker Trust of Lexington has owned the building since 1985.

In front of the bank on the corner stands a replica of the Frankfort Centennial cornerstone, marking the founding of Frankfort by General James Wilkinson on October 6, 1786. The original cornerstone was located at the end of Ann Street by the river.

State National Bank

The State National Bank offered Kentucky's first drive-in windows in 1963.

John Hampton House CIRCA 1815 — 101 WEST MAIN STREET

Tax records from the year 1818 show John Hampton owned and operated a tavern in Franklin County. Sources point to 1815 for the construction of this stone house. The dwelling was made of patterned river limestone with jack arches over both the windows and doors. This is the earliest surviving stone house in Frankfort. The building became a residential dwelling when enlarged in 1840. In the 1850s it served as a boarding house.

In 1879, Colonel H. P. Williams, sheriff of Franklin County lived here. At this house on the night of March 25, Williams entertained Kentucky Court of Appeals Judge John M. Elliott. The next day, around 1 o'clock in the afternoon, Colonel Thomas Buford of Henry County murdered the judge with a double-barreled shotgun. As Judge Elliott, who boarded at the hotel, and a friend approached the side entrance on Ann Street, Buford, dressed for hunting, called out "Judge, I believe I will go snipe hunting, won't you go along?"

Elliott replied "No." Buford then said "Well, then, won't you go and take a drink?" The judge refused and Buford shot him. As he knelt beside Elliott, Buford put his hat under his head and placed his hand on the judge's brow and said: "I'm sorry." They carried Elliott's lifeless body to a room in the hotel where a coroner's inquest took place. The judge's wife was in the hotel at the time of his death.

Buford said he killed Elliott because of a recent decision the Judge rendered against his sister involving $20,000. Authorities removed Buford to Louisville to prevent a mob from hanging him. Buford's plea of insanity at the trial held in Owen County brought him acquittal. Confined to the asylum at Anchorage, he later escaped and went to Indiana. The extradition laws at that time were not sufficient to have him returned to Kentucky.

+ + + + + + + + + + + + + + + + +

The funeral was in the First Christian Church with Reverend C.W. Miller of the Methodist Church presiding. Frankfort Mayor S. I. M. Major requested the closing of all businesses at noon. The Louisville *Courier Journal* published the funeral sermon in full.

Judge John Elliott was born in Virginia in 1820. He became a lawyer in 1841 in Floyd County, Kentucky. He served in the state legislature and in Congress for several terms. In 1861 the United States Court expelled him from the state legislature for "directly or indirectly giving aid and comfort to the enemy." Elliott then cast his fortunes with the South and served in the Confederate Congress assembled in Richmond, Virginia. After the war he returned to Kentucky and settled in Bath County where he was elected Judge of the Circuit Court.

Judge Elliott has one of the Frankfort Cemetery's most interesting monuments located in section M. On the marble base stands the Goddess of Liberty, blindfolded and holding in her hand the scales of justice.

Sign of the Cocked Hat Tavern
Rebecca-Ruth Candy once
operated from this building.

Sign of the Cocked Hat Tavern CIRCA 1860 — 100 EAST MAIN STREET

The lot for this building, lot 193, is in the shape of a tri-corn hat and in older official documents was called the "Cocked Hat Lot." The property has been in possession of some prominent people from its earliest times. Hayden Edwards, Mark Hardin, and Richard Taylor once owned it. The lot was on a plat of Frankfort in 1805. In 1815, Hayden Edwards deeded the lot to Richard Taylor who ran an inn on the southwest corner of Main and Ann Streets. Taylor may have expanded his business to this location. The entrance to the tavern was on High Street with sleeping rooms available on the second floor. A few years later Taylor bought the famous Mansion House on the northwest corner of Main and St. Clair.

Historian William J. Hearn, referring to an 1801 advertisement in a Frankfort newspaper, the *Palladium*, says the Sign of the Cocked Hat originally was an early 1800 hatting business owned by James McClean.

Construction dates for the present building were between 1854 and 1871. An 1854 map does not show the building but it does appear on a map for 1871. It was probably a combination house and business with the residential entrance on Main Street and the business entrance on High Street. The walls of stone are between eighteen and twenty-four inches thick. Rebecca-Ruth Candy once operated from this building.

State Arsenal CIRCA 1850 — 125 EAST MAIN STREET

The state's first arsenal was located on the northeast corner of the public square bounded by Lewis, Clinton, Madison and Market (Broadway) Streets. In 1834 a gun house on the square (affectionately called the Old Green House) was dismantled and the materials used to construct the first arsenal. At 3 AM on March 12, 1836, a powder explosion rocked the town and the building was destroyed by fire. Another small structure was built for temporary use until 1850 when the legislature ordered the construction of the present facility on East Main Street. The appropriation bill required that the arsenal be at least a half-mile from the state capitol for protection purposes. When the building was erected, East Main Street was on the south side of the structure. Constructed of brick on limestone foundations, the castellated style edifice has two tiers of openings, three-bayed on the ends and five on the flanks. There are square towers dividing each bay stationed at the corners.

The architect was Frankfort resident Nathaniel Cook, who had assisted in building the Good Shepherd Catholic Church on Wapping Street. He was a private in the First Kentucky Regiment of Mounted Volunteers during the Mexican War and a member of the 36th Regiment of Enrolled Militia called out in 1864 to defend Frankfort against a Confederate invasion during the Civil War.

During the first years of the Civil War the Arsenal served as a cartridge factory. Frankfort women and children made the ammunition that supplied Union troops from Kentucky, Indiana, Ohio, and Michigan. The cartridge factory ceased operation in 1862 when the Confederates took control of Frankfort for nearly a month. In 1864 the Arsenal came under enemy fire for the only time in its history. Federals exchanged shots with rebels on the opposite side of the Kentucky River.

After the Civil War, the Arsenal supplied Kentucky State Guard troops with munitions during rioting and assisted with supplies for the Spanish-American War, the Mexican Border Campaign, and the First World War. On July 30, 1933, an explosion and fire on the second floor of the arsenal destroyed approximately $150,000 worth of federal and state military property. The exterior brick walls remained intact but the building sustained $30,000 in damages.

After the Department of Military Affairs built the Boone National Guard Center in the 1970s, the Arsenal was disbanded. In 1973, the Kentucky Historical Society moved its extensive weapons collection and military relics into the Arsenal, creating the Kentucky Military History Museum. Kentucky Governor Wendell Ford dedicated the facility on February 18, 1974. Today the museum, under the auspices of the Kentucky Historical Society, preserves and maintains Kentucky's martial heritage.

During the Civil War, the arsenal came under enemy fire in 1864.

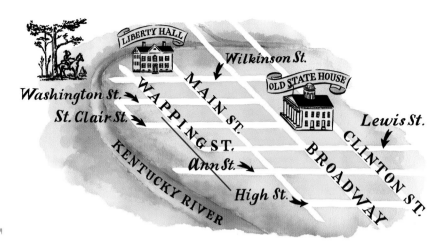

Chapter Five
ST. CLAIR STREET

St. Clair Street runs from north to south, paralleling Washington and Lewis Streets. This street was named in honor of Arthur St. Clair, a major general during the Revolutionary War and the fifteenth President of the Continental Congress. Born in Scotland in 1734, he came to America to fight in the French and Indian War. Following the war he settled in Pennsylvania with his wealthy wife and family. During the Revolution he joined Washington's army. For his valor in the battles of Trenton and Princeton, he obtained the rank of Major General in 1777. His abandonment of Fort Ticonderoga climaxed his career as a field commander. He retired from the Continental Army in 1783. St. Clair served in Congress from 1785 to 1787. President Washington appointed St. Clair the first governor of the Northwest Territory in 1789. In 1791 he was named Major General and Commander of the U.S. Army. That same year he met defeat by a combined force of Ohio Indians led by the Miami chief Little Turtle. Known in history as "St. Clair's Defeat," it was the greatest American Indian victory over any American military force. Over 800 American soldiers and camp followers were dead on the battlefield. After retiring as territorial governor, he returned to Pennsylvania becoming one of the founders of the Pittsburgh iron-making business. St. Clair was no more successful as a businessperson than he was as a general, dying in poverty in 1818.

The "Singing Bridge" CIRCA 1894

This bridge, measuring 408 feet in length, was once the longest single span structure in Kentucky. When first constructed the flooring was originally wooden. The bridge did not start to "sing" until 1938 when the open grate floor was installed. One can hear a variety of musical pitches created by the weight and speed of passing traffic, thus it is locally called the "singing" bridge. The bridge opened to vehicular traffic on March 24, 1894. During the bridge's centennial celebration, the Frankfort *State Journal* issued an article that told of the first "foot" traffic:

> Almost three weeks previous to its opening to traffic, the bridge underwent a test of sorts by Caroline Gray, the young daughter of city commissioner and local hardware merchant M.P. Gray. Miss Gray, mounted on her pony "Brownie," reportedly rode across the structure and back again "crossing at the further end by means of the footway," according to the March 4, 1894 edition of the The Capital newspaper. "Brownie weighs fully 100 pounds when Miss Caroline is mounted upon him, and competent engineers say the structure held their weight without sinking the hundreth part on an inch.

The "Singing Bridge" replaced an earlier covered bridge on the same site. The Frankfort Bridge Company incorporated December 29, 1799 to build a bridge across the river from the south end of Ann Street. However, the realization of a new bridge was slow in coming about. A pontoon bridge constructed of anchored flat boats covered with plank for the roadway and with railing on each side for protection was in operation before 1807. In 1810 an act was approved to erect a bridge across the river from the south end of St. Clair Street becoming Frankfort's first permanent bridge. It is a popular tradition that Thomas Metcalfe, later governor of Kentucky, erected one of the piers for the uncovered tollbridge. Lafayette would cross this bridge during his famous visit in 1825. The bridge underwent repair work in 1835, collapsing a few days later, carrying into the river two teams, their wagons and drivers. Of the several people crossing the bridge, two died from the fall. A new bridge replaced the old one in 1848. Persons outside the county were required to pay a toll of six and a half cents on foot or horseback and the same per head for cattle. All persons were charged fifty cents for carriages or wagons. During the horse and buggy days the bridge displayed a sign at each end threatening a fine of five dollars to anyone driving a horse faster than a walk. In 1878 the bridge was jointly purchased by the city and county for $7000 and made free from toll.

Destruction by fire threatened the old covered bridge several times. During the Civil War there was danger of destruction by invading Confederate troops. In the late 1860s, the north end of the bridge experienced severe damage when a whiskey warehouse caught fire. The whiskey barrels burst from the intense heat and the contents caught fire and ran down into the river, causing the destruction of a number of boats as well as catching the bridge on fire.

After the state of Kentucky ceded control of its rivers to the United States government, orders were received from the War Department to elevate all bridges to a certain level above the high water mark, necessitating changes to the old covered bridge. In July of 1893, city and county officials signed a contract with the King Bridge Company of Cleveland, Ohio, to construct a modern steel span costing $65,700.

During Kentucky's 1992 Bicentennial celebration, Downtown Frankfort Inc. installed special lighting for the bridge and placed historical markers at the northern end of the bridge.

First Baptist Church

Originally called "The Church of Jesus Christ at Frankfort," it took the present name First Baptist in 1898.

First Baptist Church CIRCA 1868 — 201 ST. CLAIR STREET

In 1816 several members of the Forks of Elkhorn Baptist Church organized Frankfort's First Baptist Church. John Taylor agreed to serve as temporary pastor and the church first met in the Assembly Hall, the original courthouse, as well as in people's homes. They also shared the Public House of Worship on the southwest corner of the Old Capitol grounds with the Presbyterians every fourth Sunday. Silas Noel, one of the founders of Georgetown College, preached the first sermon. While Noel would later serve as a full-time minister, the first to do so was Henry Toler. With the burning of the Public House of Worship, the Baptist congregation moved to a new building on Lewis Street not far from the southwest corner of Main. Porter Clay, younger brother of Henry Clay, was among the early pastors serving from May 1825 to October 26, 1826. He was also State Auditor of Kentucky for many years and later moved to Missouri where some sources say he gave the first sermon in English west of the Mississippi River. When the Lewis Street church burned on December 6, 1867, the congregation would move to its location at 201 St. Clair.

The first titleholder of the property, Thomas Loughbridge, built a large two-story frame house on the site. Later, Edward Payne Johnson, the owner of the first stage line between Frankfort and Louisville would live here. When the house burnt, the Baptists purchased the land and constructed the present building in 1868. The Victorian edifice combined Romanesque towers and window arches with a basic Gothic Revival form. Charles Hinds tell us in his history of the First Baptist Church that a contract for the central building was let to Leo Oberwarth, the father of architect Julian Oberwarth. The Oberwarth family designed many structures in Frankfort including the Second Street School and the State National Bank building. Renovation of the church has occurred several times over the years. The façade on the front of the church came in 1904. In its infancy, the name of the church was " The Church of Jesus Christ at Frankfort." It took its present name of First Baptist in July of 1898.

First Baptist Church made history in 2001 when it became the first church in Kentucky to vote to withdraw from the Southern Baptist Convention because of its growing conservatism and control.

Franklin County Courthouse CIRCA 1835 — ST. CLAIR STREET

Franklin County's first courthouse was on the southeast corner of the Old Capitol grounds on Broadway. To superintend the construction, the town appointed Christopher Greenup, Daniel James, and Daniel Weisiger. Completed on September 15, 1806, the courthouse was a plain brick building approximately 40 feet square with a front portico containing four brick columns and a piazza of five arches that opened on the hall for the county courts. On the same floor were the clerks' offices. The jury rooms were on the second floor and the local Hiram No. 4 Masonic Lodge added a third floor to the building for meeting purposes. John Rennick was custodian of the house and yard and was directed to plant numerous locust trees for shade. The grounds also contained a stock and whipping post.

By the early 1830s the courthouse at Broadway and Lewis Street was no longer sufficient to conduct the growing affairs of Franklin County. Local businessmen John Harris Hanna, Jeptha Dudley and J. J. Marshall donated a St. Clair Street lot to the county December 19, 1831 for the site of the new structure. Architect Gideon Shryock was the natural choice to develop the plans. His services were engaged in June of 1832 while he was working on the Morrison College building at Transylvania University in Lexington. The local supervising committee consisted of Charles S. Morehead (later Governor of Kentucky), Henry Wingate and James Shannon. Other leading citizens involved in planning the courthouse were Mason Brown and Philip Swigert. Although they finished the building at a cost of $12,500 in November 1835, it was 1840 before the bill was paid.

Set on a slight elevation, the Greek Revival building has a monumental stairway and a portico of four Doric columns. The pyramidal roof supports an octagonal belfry. The addition of the clock, purchased in Philadelphia, occurred in 1833. Originally, the first floor of the two-story limestone structure held the courtroom and the offices for sheriff and justices of the

Franklin County Courthouse

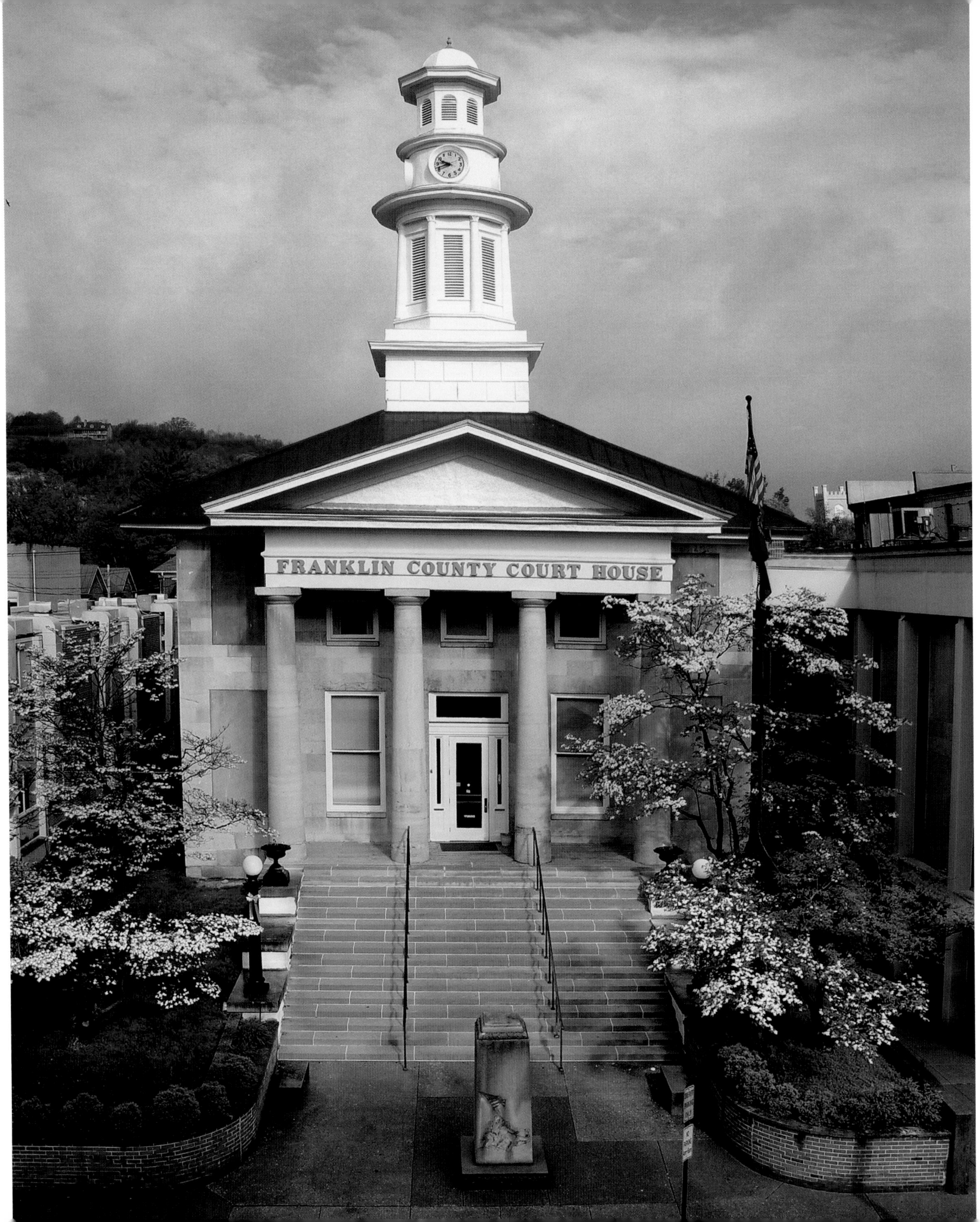

peace. Jury rooms occupied the second floor.

Extensive remodeling of the building took place in 1909 supervised by local architect Leo L. Oberwarth. Born in Brooklyn in 1872, and educated in Germany, at age 16 he moved with his family to Frankfort. Oberwarth had designed the Elks Club building in 1902 and the expansion of King's Daughters Hospital in 1904. He removed the rear of the courthouse and extended the building thirty feet. With the removal of the upper floor, additional rooms on the second floor housed the courtroom, justices' office and sheriff's office, leaving more space for court offices on the first floor. This $40,000 renovation gave the building a pagoda look.

Other changes would occur in 1927. The county court clerk's offices were rebuilt and enlarged in 1949. The addition of a north side wing came in 1970. In 1971 the building was listed on the National Register of Historic Places. Arson was blamed for a serious courthouse fire in 1995. During the fall of 2001, more renovation of the courthouse included the addition of a new copper roof and much needed belfry restoration work.

The structure was listed on the National Register of Historic Places in 1971.

Chapter Six
BROADWAY

Broadway is the widest street in Frankfort and runs parallel to Main and Clinton Streets. When first utilized it was known as Market Street. Frankfort's first market house was located on Broadway between Ann and Lewis Streets. When the railroad was built in the 1830s, the market house relocated to the southeast corner of Broadway and Ann across from the present Kentucky History Center. The market house was the forerunner of the farmer's market and the modern shopping mall. Merchants and farmers sold their goods, fresh vegetables, butter and eggs in rented stalls. The rectangular building was long and at one end had a doorway wide enough for wagons to enter and unload their wares. At the opposite end a fireplace was available for warmth in winter and potential cooking year-round. A cupola containing a large bell adorned the roof. Hours varied according to the seasons and the availability of goods. One town ordinance ruled the market would be open from sunset Tuesday until 10 a.m. Wednesday and on Friday from sunset until 10 a.m. Saturday. The first foundation was of brick laid by Harrison Blanton, but exposure to the elements damaged the foundation and threatened the safety of the entire structure. A stone foundation was far superior. Nettie Glenn, in her history of early Frankfort, suggests this is why so many of the older buildings have Kentucky River marble foundations. In the mid-1880s grocery stores replaced the open market and the building was bought by the railroad and then demolished. Most towns in the early history of our country had a market house or some similar facility.

Amos Kendall House CIRCA 1810-1820 — 413 WEST BROADWAY

Today, few people in Frankfort are familiar with Amos Kendall. Born in Massachusetts, and educated at Dartmouth, Kendall arrived in Kentucky walking the 64 miles between Maysville and Lexington to become the private tutor of Henry Clay's children. He moved from Lexington to Georgetown and started a newspaper. In 1814 he went to the Court of Appeals in Frankfort to obtain a license to become a lawyer. Kendal operated a bookstore in Frankfort and was editor of the newspaper *Argus of Western America* for fifteen years. Kendall also owned a paper mill that he sold to the Stedman brothers in the 1830s when he began his association with Andrew Jackson. His skills as a newspaperman helped secure Jackson's victory in the 1828 presidential election. At Jackson's request, he moved to Washington, D.C., starting the famous *Globe* newspaper, and became a powerful member of Jackson's "Kitchen Cabinet." He was fourth auditor of the U.S. Treasury, and served as U.S. Postmaster General from 1835 to 1840. Kendall was responsible for Frankfort's Francis Preston Blair moving to Washington and taking over the editorship of the *Globe*. The popular Blair House, across from the White House, was the home of this long ago citizen of Frankfort.

In 1845 Kendall obtained extreme wealth as the business agent for Samuel Morse, the inventor of the telegraph. Kendall's fortune enabled him to devote time to writing and philanthropy. He helped found a school for the deaf and mute that evolved into Gallaudet College. With $100,000, Kendall rebuilt Calvary Baptist Church in Washington, D.C. after a devastating fire.

Amos Kendall died in 1869 at the age of eighty and his body lies buried in Washington, D.C. In Kendall's autobiography he wrote: "I have, I think, learnt the way to be popular in Kentucky, but do not as yet put it into practice. Drink whiskey and talk loud with the fullest confidence, and you will hardly fail of being called a clever fellow."

In the early 1970s, the structure underwent extensive renovation, installing heating and air conditioning and restoring fireplaces.

George Mortimer Bibb Law Office CIRCA 1824 — 333 WEST BROADWAY

The career of George Mortimer (or Motier) Bibb spanned the first half of the nineteenth century. He was both a witness to and a participant in most of the important political and legal events of his age. He was a lawyer of great prominence on the state and federal level, judge of the highest state court, twice U.S. senator, and served as Secretary of the U.S. Treasury. His Frankfort home on Washington Street no longer exists. Alice E. Trabue's "A Corner in Celebrities" relates that it was an old-fashioned two-story house with a quaint New England entrance. It was located adjacent to his brother-in-law Francis Preston Blair's house on the east side of Washington Street between the Church of Ascension and Broadway. An 1824 tax record lists this property at 333 Broadway in the ownership of George M. Bibb. His younger brother John, famous for developing Bibb lettuce, resided nearby on Wapping Street.

Bibb was born in 1776 in Prince Edward County, Virginia. He moved to Lexington, Kentucky in 1789. Establishing a successful career in law, he married a daughter of Charles Scott, later governor of Kentucky. In the early 1800s he served as Grand Master of the Grand Lodge of Kentucky Free Masons. Bibb served in the state legislature, succeeding Henry Clay in 1806. In 1808 he was commissioned a Judge of the Kentucky Court of Appeals and in the next year was designated by his father-in-law, Governor Scott, as Chief Justice of Kentucky. He became U.S. Senator in 1811 and was among the "War Hawks" pushing for war with Great Britain.

Following a second term as U.S. Senator from Kentucky, Bibb was appointed to the Louisville Chancery Court and thus acquired the title "Chancellor," by which he was generally known in later life. His friendship with John Tyler during his service in the Jackson administration culminated in his appointment as U.S. Secretary of the Treasury in the summer of 1844.

In his latter years, he was a reminder of a bygone era. He was the last to wear the old style knee britches in Washington. In 1859 he died of pneumonia at his home near Washington, D.C. and is buried there.

Bibb was the last congressman in Washington to wear the old-style knee britches.

Old State Capitol

Old State Capitol CIRCA 1830 — BROADWAY AT ST. CLAIR

Frankfort, the state capital of Kentucky, will forever be indebted to Andrew Holmes. When Kentucky obtained statehood in 1792, the first legislature met in the market house building on Lexington's Main Street not far from the Fayette County courthouse. The legislature selected Frankfort over Lexington, Louisville, Petersburg, and Leestown, not only because of its choice location on the Kentucky River but primarily due to the efforts of Andrew Holmes. In the early 1790s the fledgling town of Frankfort contained several cabins, some warehouses, and a few inns. Holmes, with eight Frankfort businessmen, realizing that a greater population was needed to insure the town's commercial development, submitted a proposal to build Kentucky's first permanent capitol in Frankfort. This proposal offered the state a home formerly occupied by General James Wilkinson, several city lots including the public square, materials to build the statehouse, and a sum of $3000 in specie. The Wilkinson house was located on the southwest corner of Wilkinson and Wapping Streets. This was the first structure used by the legislature in Frankfort. Holmes Street bears the named of this enterprising man, who died in 1803.

The present "Old State Capitol" is the third building on this site. Fire destroyed the first two capitols in 1813 and 1824. The legislature approved the third capitol with a bill that appropriated $20,000 in money and supplies. The building commissioners appointed were some of Frankfort's leading citizens: John Brown, Daniel Weisiger, Peter Dudley, John J. Crittenden, John Harvie, Evan Evans and James Shannon. They chose an architectural plan from Gideon Shryock of Lexington, the state's first native-born, professionally trained architect. When completed in 1830, this structure became the first Greek Revival statehouse west of the Alleghenies. It was built for around $90,000.

"Birds eye limestone" was used in the construction of the building. The term "birds eye" came from the small specks found in the stone that looked like the eye of a bird. Harrison Blanton provided the stone. Joel Scott, keeper of the penitentiary, invented a steam-powered sawmill to cut through the rough limestone taken from the Kentucky River. The building was to be as nearly fireproof as possible. The Ionic columns of marble are 4 feet in diameter and 33 feet high, supporting a pediment and an entablature that continues around the building. The capitol, with its portico, is 132 feet long and 70 feet wide. The whole of the roof and the dome is of copper. A dome surmounted the cupola with a lantern 22 feet in diameter and 20 feet high.

The first floor contained committee rooms and a library, with courtrooms in the rear. The second floor held the Senate and the House of Representatives. The self-supporting stone stairway in the center was one of the architectural wonders of its day. The solid upper landing served as the keystone. On a later visit Charles Shryock, Gideon's son, said that his father called attention "to the third or fourth step on the right hand flight on the outer string. He said it was cracked by an accident before the false work was removed." His father reportedly said that if the keystone shifted one-sixteenth of an inch, the entire structure would fall.

Daniel Boone and his wife Rebecca lay in state here in 1845 before their re-interment in the Frankfort Cemetery. During the Civil War, this was the only loyal state capitol building in the United States captured by Confederate

Old State Capitol

Old State Capitol

This was the only loyal state capital building in the United States captured by Confederate forces.

forces. On January 30, 1900, candidate for governor William Goebel was assassinated as he walked to the front door. The building was Kentucky's Capitol until 1910, when the new capitol was erected across the river in south Frankfort. The Old Capitol served as a government shirt depot during the days of World War I. The Kentucky Historical Society utilized the building as its headquarters and museum from 1920 until moving into the new Kentucky History Center in 1999. Today the building serves as a public museum reflecting its use as the statehouse during the 1850s.

First Railroad West of the Alleghenies CIRCA 1834

In 1830 the Lexington and Ohio Railroad chartered a rail line from Lexington to Louisville. It was an attempt by the city of Lexington to overcome the disadvantages of not being on a river. Steamboat traffic on the Ohio River had made Louisville the state's premier urban community. Frankfort would benefit from this effort due to its geographical location between the two bigger cities. The track was completed to Frankfort on January 31, 1834.

The first depot was located between the Frankfort Cemetery and what is now Kentucky State University. Freight was loaded onto two-wheeled drays that delivered the goods downtown. Passengers had the choice of taking a cab into town or riding a windlass-controlled car down the incline to the bottom of the hill. Construction debts and other financial problems brought a halt to further advancement of the rail line. At one point it had the reputation of being the worst built railroad in the nation.

Originally the rails were laid upon stone sills that were hollowed out in the middle so that the flanges of the wheels would run in the channel, holding the car on the track. There were no "ties" for the tracks such as we know today. The rails were merely strips of iron three inches broad and about one-half inch thick. During excavation work for the new Church of the Good Shepherd on U.S. 421, the Frankfort *State Journal* reported builders uncovered some limestone sills in their original location along the L & O route from Lexington to Frankfort. The first trains were horse-drawn but by 1835 were replaced by the steam locomotive. By locomotive, the four-hour trip between Lexington and Frankfort would be reduced to two hours and twenty-nine minutes.

Passenger cars were only about twelve feet long with two wheels under each end. The car was enclosed and on the roof there was a double seat with passengers sitting back to back. To protect passengers from the weather as well as from showering cinders and coals, a canopy or awning was constructed overhead. The first steam locomotive was the Lexington-built "Daniel Boone," capable of attaining the speed of 12 miles an hour. Frequent accidents happened on the road generally caused by the loosening of the rails. In 1836 a serious mishap occurred about two miles east of town. The locomotive derailed from an embankment killing three people and injuring the rest of the passengers.

In 1842 the Kentucky Legislature voted to repair the railroad in the interest of the taxpayers. The next year the legislature leased the railroad to local businessmen for $20,000. The railroad line from Lexington to Louisville was completed in 1851. The excavation of a tunnel and the re-routing of the railroad eliminated the treacherous descent into downtown Frankfort. The construction of a stronger bridge across the Kentucky River at Frankfort provided the heavy locomotives safe passage crossing the river.

By the early 1900s, Frankfort was served by four railroad companies: the Louisville and Nashville, the Chesapeake and Ohio, the Highland Railway and the Frankfort and Cincinnati (formerly the Kentucky Midland Railway). In 1908 the L & N built a new depot on the south side of Broadway between Ann and High Streets, but when passenger service ended in the early 1970s, the depot became office space. The L & N constructed a new $600,000 railroad bridge across the Kentucky River at the west end of Broadway in 1929.

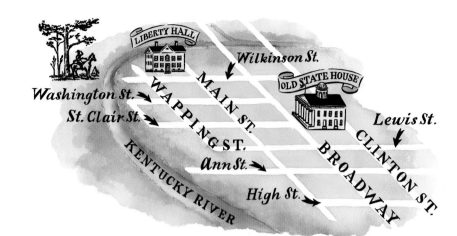

Chapter Seven
ANN STREET

Ann Street affectionately referred to as "Annie" Street in the early days, was named for the wife of Frankfort's founder, James Wilkinson. Ann Biddle Wilkinson was born to a wealthy banking family in Philadelphia. Wilkinson met her while pursuing his education in Philadelphia. They married in 1778 and had three sons: John, James and Joseph. The latter was born in Lexington, where they had settled in 1785. Besides being an army officer, her husband was involved in land speculation, salt mining, milling, medicine, and politics. Wilkinson also opened the second department store in Lexington. Ann Wilkinson was beloved by her husband's troops, not only for her beauty, but also for her kindness and concern for them. Following a move to New Orleans, Ann succumbed to tuberculosis and died in 1807.

The survey of the town began at the foot of Ann Street where the old levee was located. This was the landing for the ferryboat. Traces of old stone steps are still in evidence at the end of the street. An account found in the files of the Kentucky Historical Society says that here in 1780 Captain William Bryan and a party of friends, while fording the river, were attacked by Indians. One of Bryan's men, Stephen Frank, was killed, and that area became known as "Frank's Ford," later rendered " Frankfort." Other accounts say the event occurred near present day Taylor Avenue at the intersection of Devil's Hollow Road, or it may have happened near the present day Frankfort High School gymnasium on Ewing Street. Historian Willard Rouse Jillson believed it was at the mouth of Benson Creek.

Masonic Lodge #4 F & AM
CIRCA 1893 — 308 ANN STREET

In 1893 one of Louisville's leading architectural firms, Clarke and Loomis, erected this Romanesque Bedford limestone structure. This is a most interesting building with its symbolic and whimsical carvings illustrative of the Freemason art. Architect Charles Julian Clarke (1836-1908) was born in Franklin County to Joseph and Harriet (Julian) Clarke. Arthur Loomis of Massachusetts entered the firm in 1876 and became Clarke's chief draftsman in 1885. Clarke is buried in the Frankfort Cemetery.

In 1799 the Grand Lodge of Virginia granted a charter to constitute Hiram Lodge in Frankfort. Daniel Weisiger was its first Master, Thomas Todd was first senior warden and Baker Ewing was the first junior warden. Weisiger was an earlier county clerk, postmaster, and operated one of the most recognized houses of entertainment in the West on the northeast corner of Main and Ann Streets. Judge Todd was Chief Justice of the Court of Appeals, and later appointed by President Thomas Jefferson as United States Supreme Court Justice. Ewing was the first Registrar of the Land Office.

The first lodge room was on the third floor of the original Franklin County Courthouse located on the southeast corner of Broadway and Lewis Streets. When the old courthouse was demolished, the lodge moved to the third floor of a building on Main Street across from the present State National Bank. The first floor was used as a fire engine house. The next move found the lodge in a building on Ann Street near the railroad. When fire destroyed this location, they moved to St. Clair Street. For a time they met in the north hall of the Odd Fellows Temple and on the third floor of the *Yeoman* newspaper building. A permanent home resulted in the building at this location on Ann Street. The YMCA used the second floor until building its own facility at the southwest end of the Singing Bridge.

Frankfort's Philip Swigert entered the Grand Lodge in 1820 and served for half a century. At various times he was Senior Grand Deacon, Grand Treasurer, Grand Secretary, Junior Grand Warden, Senior Grand Warden and Most Worshipful Grand Master. For 45 years he was Grand Secretary of the Grand Chapter of the Royal Arch Masons.

Early membership reads like a who's who in the history of Frankfort. Besides those already mentioned, members included: George W. Lewis, William A. Gaines, E H. Taylor, Ebenezer Stedman, Daniel W. Lindsey, John Mason Brown, Harry Innes Todd, S.I.M. Major, John Marshall Harlan, George B. Macklin, and John W. Russell.

First Christian Church CIRCA 1872 — 316 ANN STREET

In the early 1800s "Raccoon" John Smith attempted to start a Christian church in Frankfort. None of the local churches would permit him the use of their pulpit so he secured the courthouse on the southeast corner of Broadway. Johnson's *History of Franklin County* tells us his text was "… when John came to Frankfort his spirit was stirred within him when he saw the city wholly given up to sectarianism." Smith held regular services in the old courthouse and later at the residence of John L. Moore. The Frankfort Christian Church was organized by Philip Slater Fall and John T. Johnson December 2, 1832. Charter members included P. S. Fall, his wife Nancy Bacon Fall, Elizabeth Bacon, Ambrose W. Dudley, Eliza G. Dudley, Elias B. Myers, and O. L. Leonard. For a short time services were held in the new Franklin County Courthouse. In 1842, members built their first church at a cost of $4,531.31. The sanctuary was separated into two vestibules, one for men and one for women, each with its own front door. This mode of worship continued until 1853.

In the early morning hours of November 2, 1870, a fire started on St. Clair Street and worked its way down Broadway to Lewis Street. The fire department utilized every piece of equipment it had but it was not enough. High winds fanned the fire toward the cupola of the First Christian Church, engulfing the building in flames. In the wake of the fire, more than two dozen business and residential structures suffered losses totaling $113,000. After two years the church was re-built at a cost of nearly $27,000, a gift to the congregation by Emily Thomas Tubman, who grew up in Frankfort and married a wealthy Georgia planter. Members dedicated the restored building August 11, 1872.

Among the more famous preachers who held protracted meetings for First Christian were Barton W. Stone, Alexander Campbell and Jacob Creath, Sr. Philip Slater Fall ministered without compensation for over 25 years at First Christian Church. His main source of income came from his Female Eclectic Institute and an earlier girls' school, located three miles north of Frankfort. Another much-loved preacher was George Darsie, who also served nearly 25 years.

Albert Bacon Fall had a passion for books and learning instilled by his grandfather, Philip S. Fall. Born at Frankfort in 1861, Fall was named for his uncle Albert Boult Fall, a Confederate soldier killed at Fort Donelson. His father, Williamson Ware Robertson Fall, had served in Nathan Bedford Forrest's Confederate cavalry. Albert was raised by his grandparents, living only occasionally with his parents. He attended First Christian Church and taught school at Bald Knob. Influenced by Judge William Lindsay, he studied law. He went west searching for gold, becoming a cattle hand. As a lawyer he defended constable John Selman who

was charged with killing John Wesley Hardin. He also represented an accused assassin in the killing of Sheriff Pat Garrett. He aided in writing the constitution of the state of New Mexico and later became U.S. Senator from that state.

While serving in Congress Fall became friends with Ohio senator Warren G. Harding. When Harding became President, he asked Fall to be his Secretary of State. Instead, Fall became Minister of the Interior in Harding's cabinet. A. B. Fall's involvement with the "Teapot Dome" scandal brought accusations of bribery culminating in a year's imprisonment and a $100,000 fine. Harding said: "If Albert Fall isn't an honest man, I'm not fit to be President of the United States." Due to poor health he served only 9 months and 19 days of his prison sentence. In 1944, at age 83, three years after his prison release, he died in obscurity in a Santa Fe hospital.

John Haly House

John Haly House CIRCA 1860 — 410-412 ANN STREET

John Haly was born in Ireland around 1827. Twenty years later he came to America and settled in Boston, finding employment at the Boston Water Works for two years. Before arriving in Frankfort in the early 1850s, Haly had lived in Albany, New York and in Cincinnati, Ohio. While in Cincinnati he worked for architect Isaiah Rogers, who developed the plans for building Frankfort's magnificent Capital Hotel. John Haly, hired as builder, razed the famous Weisiger Inn and within ten months had the hotel ready for the December legislature of 1853.

Over the next forty years he would serve as the city's premier builder. At first he lived on Washington Street near Clinton. Around 1860 Haly built his own home on the site of the First Methodist Church that burned in 1854. Haly's family lived on the right side and Ephraim L. Van Winkle, Secretary of State under Governor Thomas Bramlette, occupied the left side. The structure is thought to be the last Greek Revival home built in north Frankfort. His offices were located to the right of the original Farmer's Bank building at Main and Lewis Streets.

Haly was Frankfort's premier builder for over 40 years.

When Frankfort planned the centennial celebration in 1886 Haly was asked to provide an account of his building activities since arriving in town. His response (in possession of the Kentucky Historical Society) shares much information about buildings in and around Frankfort:

1850 — The Good Shepherd Parish on Wapping Street
1853 — The Capital Hotel
1854 — The Gas House at the southeast corner of Washington and Mero Street
1855 — The Farmers Bank at Main and Lewis Street
　　　　The north block of stores between 206 and 212 West Main Street
1856 — The north block of stores between 222 and 238 West Main Street
1857 — The Henry Clay Monument, Lexington Cemetery
1858 — The Daniel Boone Monument, Frankfort Cemetery (may be 1862)
　　　　The Lawrenceburg Courthouse
1860 — The Lancaster Courthouse
　　　　The Kentucky Military Institute (Stewart Home School)
　　　　The corner building at 201 West Main Street
1868 — The Frankfort Fire Department Engine House at 307 West Main Street
　　　　The original Second Street School 3-story building
1869 — The building on the south west corner of Main and Ann Street
1871 — The Old Capitol Annex
1879 — The Cedar Cove Water Works new reservoir wall
1883 — The Capital Theatre-City Hall on Main Street (razed 1979)

John Haly also built banks in Harrodsburg, Nicholasville, Georgetown, Henderson, Somerset, Russellville, and Louisville (Actor's Theatre). He built churches in Lawrenceburg and Louisville, St. Catherine's Academy in Lexington and St.Mary's College in Marion County, Kentucky. In 1876 he was contracted to build the governor's stables in Frankfort. In 1877 he remodeled the old Solomon P. Sharp house on Madison Street (razed in the 1970s to make room for the John C. Watts Federal Building).

Haly died at age 64 on October 27, 1890 and was buried in the Frankfort Cemetery.

John W. Cannon House CIRCA 1866 — 418-420 ANN STREET

Riverboat captain John W. Cannon was born in Hancock County, Kentucky in 1820. Fifty years later he would become the most famous man in America at the time. At nineteen years of age he went to New Orleans and started his career in steam boating. Over the years he built, owned, and commanded fifteen large sidewheel steamboats. Before the Civil War he began building this house on Ann Street but it was not finished until 1866. His wife Louisa was a granddaughter of Reverend Philip Slater Fall, one of the founders of Frankfort's First Christian Church. A son, John Stout Cannon, was married to one of the early directors of research for the Kentucky Historical Society, Jouett Taylor.

National notoriety came to John Cannon on July 4, 1870 when his steamboat *Robert E. Lee* defeated the *Natchez* in a Mississippi River race between New Orleans and St. Louis. The nearly 1200 miles was covered in 3 days, 18 hours and about 30 minutes. Three separate accounts give three different times for the minutes. Regardless of the exact time, no other boat race created so much interest. Thousands lined the waterfronts to see the boats pass. At night the riverbanks were ablaze with campfires. The *Natchez* required 4 days and 51 minutes to finish.

The *Lee* was constructed at Jeffersonville, Indiana, in 1866 at a cost of nearly $250,000. When it was discovered that the boat would be named for General Lee, public feeling was so negative that threats were made to burn it. Cannon moved the unfinished boat to the Portland wharf at Louisville where it was completed. The *Natchez* was built at Cincinnati and was launched in 1869. Its captain, also a native Kentuckian, was Tom P. Leathers of Covington.

The race between the steamers came about through a rivalry that grew out of their competition for trade on the lower Mississippi. On different days of the week both boats ran on a regular basis between New Orleans and Vicksburg carrying huge shipments of cotton. With supremacy of the river on the line, it was inevitable that the boats would race. Both steamers had the support of many friends and the rival captains finally agreed to a race. The two captains made no wagers and there was no "purse" or monetary reward for the winner. The only thing at stake was honor on the river.

In the early days of Frankfort, steamboats were built at the mouth of Steamboat Hollow just north of town. An early Lexington newspaper, the *Kentucky Gazette*, reported, "the first sea vessel built at Frankfort has been captured at sea by English frigates." The vessel, *Go By*, sailing from Santo Domingo to Curacco, was captured November 7, 1804 by the English ship *Diana*. The *Go By* was built by John Instone who lived on the site of the Bibb house on Wapping Street.

In 1995 on the 125th anniversary of the "Great Steamboat Race," modern day riverboats recreated the famous race to honor Cannon, featuring the *Delta Queen* and its sister ship, the *Mississippi Queen. Delta Queen* officials say Cannon's record still stands, since the contest that year was somewhat slower, involving an 11-day cruise.

Captain John Cannon died April 18, 1882 and lies buried in the Frankfort cemetery.

John W. Cannon House

Mary Train Runyan House CIRCA 1844 — 518 ANN STREET

Before public education was available in Frankfort in the mid-1860s, private schooling was the main source of student learning. The oldest private school still in operation in Frankfort is Good Shepherd School. In 1860 the Sisters of Charity opened Saint Joseph Academy, located on the present site of the Frankfort Police Station on Second Street. The first major private school in Frankfort was the Kentucky Seminary, directed by Kean O'Hara on the site of today's Old Capitol Annex. The 1840s generated other private academies such as Reverend Philip Slater Fall's Female Eclectic Institute, Burwell Bassett Sayre's Institute for Boys, and Mary Train Runyan's Greenwood Female Seminary. Following the Civil War other well-known private schools included the Dudley Institute and the Excelsior Collegiate Institute.

In 1844 at age 24, Mrs. Runyan opened her school for girls. The actual school site was located next door at the southwest corner of Ann and Mero Streets. The Greek Revival common bond brick building at 518 Ann was her residence. It also served as a boarding house for young women who often came from a great distance to attend the school. Eventually the school would become co-educational. The Greenwood Seminary was renowned in central Kentucky until Mrs. Runyan closed the school upon the death of her husband in the late 1800s.

Mrs. Runyan was thoroughly educated and especially fitted to assist young students in their education. Her school was always limited to a certain number of students. She cared for her pupils morally, physically, as well as intellectually. A graduate of the Greenwood School was self-reliant and self-sustaining. The curriculum at the seminary compared favorably with that of any school in the country. A rare feature was that of calisthenics. The following was a typical advertisement for the school in the December 1853 edition of Frankfort's *Tri-Weekly Commonwealth*.

GREENWOOD FEMALE SEMINARY

Mrs. M.T. Runyan, Prin.

Miss M. G. Biglow, Asst.

**The eleventh session of this school will commence on
The second Monday in Jan. (Jan. 9, 1854)**

Terms Per Session of 20 Weeks

Board, including washing, fuel and lights	**$50.00**
Primary Department	10.00
Second Junior Department	12.00
First Junior Department	6.00
Senior Department	20.00
Latin or French (each)	10.00
Drawing and Painting	10.00
Music on Piano or Guitar	3.00
Stationery	25.00
Plain or ornamental needlework without charge	

Frankfort, Kentucky   Dec. 26, 1853

Mary Train Runyan died four days following her 81st birthday in 1901. She is buried in the Frankfort Cemetery.

This residence also served as a boarding house for young women who attended the Greenwood Seminary.

S. I. M. Major Jr. House CIRCA 1835 — 519 ANN STREET

In the 1830s, Commodore of the United States Navy William S. Harris owned this property site. Harris was married to Sarah Ann Sneed, the daughter of Achilles Sneed who lived on adjoining property. The house was built by Alfred Z. Boyer, and upon his death was used as a boarding house by his widow. S. I. M. Major Sr. bought it in 1852 and upon his death, ownership transferred to his son. The property was considered for the Governor's Mansion and Capitol grounds. In 1886, Major sold the home to State Auditor Carl Norman who added several tenant houses. The house would remain in the Norman family for 84 years. Norman also served Kentucky as State Senator, major in the Confederate Army under General John Hunt Morgan and as State Insurance Commissioner.

The main house encompasses more than 7,000 square feet of living space. There is a three-floor staircase with accompanying hand-carved walnut banister. Six massive columns once supported the second-story balcony. There are 12 open fireplaces. Double parlors extend on the left side of a huge hallway. On the right side of the hallway was a library that opened into the dining room. The second floor contained a master bedroom, nursery, and two other bedrooms. The Major family had several children who died before reaching the age of four. Frank Sower, in his *Reflections on Frankfort*, suggests we may have another haunted house in Frankfort besides Liberty Hall. According to Sower, legend has it that at night one can hear the crying of children coming from the nursery. Retired curator of the Governor's Mansion, Juett Sheetinger, bought the property in 1970 from the Norman family.

Samuel Ire Monger Major Jr. was born near Frankfort in 1830. He was one of the best-educated men in Frankfort, taught by the illustrious Burwell Basset Sayre, one of the most popular teachers in Kentucky. For a short time he found employment as a surveyor and a schoolteacher. In 1852 he became associated with one of Frankfort's most memorable newspapers, *The Kentucky Yeoman*. Major was proprietor and editor of the paper until it suspended operation in 1886. During his editorship, the *Yeoman* was the leading Democratic newspaper in the state. He held the state office of Public Printer and Binder for many years due to the power of his newspaper.

Major married Mary B. Scott, daughter of attorney and successful farmer Robert Wilmot Scott and granddaughter of Dr. Preston Brown, younger brother of Senator John Brown. Her father, Robert, was noted for being the first in the area to introduce Cashmere and Angora sheep at his farm known today as "Scotland" near Jett in eastern Franklin County. Scott died at his son-in-law's home here on Ann Street in 1886.

Major was one of Frankfort's most distinguished public servants. Not only did he serve his community as mayor four straight terms, but was in the state legislature twice. As mayor, he was greatly instrumental in establishing the public school system. The Major Hall theatre, and Major Street, were both named for him. Major Hall provided only a few months of theatrical entertainment at its Main Street location before it was destroyed by fire.

Major hired other editors to work for the *Yeoman* including famed poet Theodore O'Hara and Colonel Walter W. Stapp, the founder of the old Louisville *Times*. During Major's reign as editor, he was frequently in personal danger. Writing about political opponents would often bring down violent wrath. On occasion, Major was obliged to carry pistols and a Bowie knife for his protection. For two years he was unable to leave his house without fear of assassination. One article in 1857 resulted in rival newspaper editor Thomas M. Green challenging Major to a duel. While the duel never took place, the consequence of having accepted the challenge was to disfranchise Major for five years. Beriah Magoffin, as one of his last acts as Governor of Kentucky, pardoned Major in 1862.

In 1876, the *Kentucky Yeoman* moved to a new building on St. Clair Street across from the Franklin County Courthouse. An interesting shield-shaped tablet of Kentucky marble, weighing 1700 pounds, raised to a central place in front of the building, bore the inscription:

KENTUCKY YEOMAN

MAJOR, JOHNSON & BARRETT

1840-1876

Kentucky Yeoman Building Monument

Years later the building was razed and the "tablet" removed to the side yard of Barrett's residence on Campbell Street where it remained a topic of conversation to passers-by for over 100 years.

S. I. M. Major is buried in the Frankfort Cemetery.

Chapter Eight
LEWIS STREET

Lewis Street gets it name from one of the great frontier Indian fighters who opened Kentucky to settlement: General Andrew Lewis. Even during his early years in Virginia he exhibited an innate readiness for authority and command. In 1729 after killing his landlord in a quarrel, his father John Lewis, a native of Ireland, fled to Virginia. John brought with him three sons, Thomas, William and Andrew.

Andrew Lewis was one of the leading defenders of the early frontier. He commanded a company in the Continental army and was wounded at Fort Necessity. He served in the Cherokee War and with Bouquet on the Muskingum. His triumph came during Lord Dunmore's War when he led Virginia troops in a fierce five-hour battle with the Shawnee at Point Pleasant in 1774. Charles Lewis, a younger brother, died in this battle. Serving with him was Evan Shelby and his young son Isaac, later to become Kentucky's first governor. Though the battle with Chief Cornstalk and the Shawnee was actually a draw, it was a victory for Kentucky. It resulted in the 1775 peace treaty at Camp Charlotte in Ohio and the Indians promised to hunt no more in Kentucky and to molest no one on the Ohio River. While this did not prevent hostilities between the settlers and the Indians, it did provide a lull in the fighting and opened the door allowing access to Kentucky. This is one of the most significant aspects of the Battle of Point Pleasant.

At first, Lewis Street was only along the east side of the Old Capitol square, and at each end of the street, it was called Buffalo Alley. In 1818 the Legislature passed an act to add sixteen feet to the west side of Buffalo Alley from Broadway to Main calling it Lewis Street.

Taylor-Compton House CIRCA 1832 — 419 LEWIS STREET

At one time this was the only house on the square bounded by Lewis, Clinton, Ann and Broadway. It was built by hand over several years by Frankfort merchant Joseph Taylor around 1832. Tax records for 1810 show Elizabeth Love once owned a building on this site. She is probably the same Elizabeth Love who, with Liberty Hall's Margaretta Mason Brown, started the first Sunday school west of the Allegheny Mountains. At the death of Joseph Taylor in 1835 the two story Federal style Flemish bond brick home became the property of his daughter, Sarah Ann, and later her husband Joseph I. Belt. Belt's father, Joseph Sr., was a veteran of the Revolutionary War and died at age 99 in 1850. Joseph Jr., was the owner of the O. and J. Belt business that started in 1831 on the site of the old Farmers Bank building at the corner of Lewis and Main Streets. After Sarah's death in 1856 the property was sold to John Moore and then to Lewis Crutcher. The latter sold it to Dr. James A. Hatchitt, brother-in-law of John Marshall Harlan, Chief Justice of the United States Supreme Court. Harlan lived on the northwest corner of Madison and Broadway across from the west side of the Old Capitol.

Hatchitt was appointed to serve as Frankfort postmaster in 1866. In the late 1860s he sold the garden section of the property to the famous riverboat captain, John Cannon, who built a large house on the southwest corner of Ann and Clinton Streets. About the same time he also sold the stable section to Captain Sanford Goin who built his home at the southeast corner of Lewis and Clinton Streets. After Hatchitt died in 1882, the property came into the possession of the Lutkemeier family.

German-born William C. Lutkemeier purchased the Taylor House in March 1885. The family started a prosperous dry goods store near the southwest corner of Lewis and Broadway in the late 1860s. The store survived three generations until closing in the early 1960s. Lutkemeier sold everything from garden seeds to horse and barn equipment. One could find a milk pail, bread, silverware, and dishes. On Saturday it was standing room only. It became the place to be in the early 1900s as rural and town folk alike would fill the aisles and while away the day.

In the late 1890s, Lutkemeier added the present dining room and an upper bedroom with a tin ceiling. In the late 1970s, a bed and breakfast was located here. In July 1989 after extensive renovation, new owner Barri Christian also offered a bed and breakfast here.

The house is named for the original builder, Joseph Taylor, and the deceased son of Ms. Christian.

The Lutkemeier family owned a famous dry goods store for over 100 years in Frankfort.

Sanford Goin Home CIRCA 1872 — 425 LEWIS STREET

Frankfort iceman, Sanford Goin, built this two-story frame residence for $4000 in 1872. Before residing at this location, he lived in an old frame house on the corner of St. Clair and Mero Streets and owned an adjacent house on Mero Street. When his daughters married, he deeded the houses to them and built the house on Lewis Street where he would reside until his death. For several years he ran a boarding house here. Advertisements in the *Kentucky Yeoman* for the Eagle Boarding House called attention to the fine food and excellent location across from the Capitol.

Goin was born in Woodford County around 1814 and moved with his parents to Frankfort in 1820. He and his brother Isom once ran a ferry across the Kentucky River just below the mouth of Benson Creek. In 1837 he purchased property in South Frankfort including all of Conway Street for the amazing price of $3.00! Goin was among the men who excavated the Cedar Cove Spring Reservoir for the Frankfort Water Company in 1838. In the early 1850s Goin went to California in search of gold. Failing to find his fortune he returned to Frankfort and began experimenting with trees. For shade trees, he found the best to be water maples. Beginning in 1855 he would plant them all over Frankfort.

Goin's finest hour was during his service as a member of Captain A. J. Graham's Company B, First Battalion, 36th Enrolled Militia, called out by Kentucky governor Thomas Bramlette in 1864 in defense of the Capital during a Confederate raid by

Sanford Goin Home

The City of Frankfort awarded Goin a sword for his participation in the defense of the town from Fort Hill during the Civil War.

some of John Hunt Morgan's men. As a reward Goin was presented with a beautiful sword of superior workmanship and finish. On the blade was inscribed:

"Presented to Captain Sanford Goins, Company H, 1st Kentucky Capital Guards, by the Citizens of Frankfort and members of his Company, for gallant conduct in the defence of Frankfort, June 10, 1864."

Nicky Hughes, City Curator of Frankfort's Historic Sites, has written:

"…Almost no one understood the critical role in Frankfort's history played by Fort Boone and its defenders. Had Morgan's men entered the city, there can be little doubt of the fate awaiting any structure associated with state government and the Union Army. The men with Morgan on this raid were hardly the "beau sabreurs" of the earlier years. Their behavior elsewhere indicates that they would have been liberal with the use of the torch, burning Frankfort buildings like those that they did warehouses in Lexington and houses in Cynthiana. Frankfort's main source of prosperity in later years – state government – would have been left in ruins…The state almost certainly would have departed for Louisville, Lexington, or elsewhere with the Old Capitol and other public square buildings, the State Arsenal, and the many houses and structures in town associated with the military government all in ashes…The citizens of Frankfort owe much to the militiamen of Fort Boone…"

At his death, Sanford Goin was buried in the Frankfort Cemetery.

Chapter Nine
CLINTON STREET

Clinton Street runs west to east from Wilkinson on past High Street. In the early days of settlement this street was the original "Buffalo Lane" up to its intersection with High. In 1845 the street was paved and graded from Washington Street to the river. The street was named to honor General George Clinton, a friend of Frankfort's founder, James Wilkinson. General Clinton was New York's first governor and served for eighteen years. He was the uncle of DeWitt Clinton, another Governor of New York. George Clinton was born in Ulster County, New York, in 1739. He was elected to the Continental Congress in 1775 and voted for the Declaration of Independence. He was a brigadier general during the Revolutionary War, and served as Vice President under Thomas Jefferson during his second term and Vice President under James Madison. He died in office April 20, 1812.

St. John African Methodist Episcopal Church CIRCA 1892 — 210 CLINTON STREET

During the beginning of the 1800s, Frankfort worship services were attended by both whites and blacks in the same building. Slaves would often accompany their owner's families. However, once inside, the congregations practiced segregation. In Carl Kramer's excellent history of Frankfort *Capital on the Kentucky*, we find in the 1830s that white Baptists "…decided it would be preferable if blacks worshipped on their own."

In 1839 black Methodists started what would become the AME Church in a small building facing Lewis Street not far from the present structure. A white woman, Mrs. Triplette, donated the property. Two of her servants, Benjamin Hunley and Benjamin Dunmore, were members of this congregation. In 1840 Reverend George Harlan became the first minister. In 1891, while Reverend D. S. Bentley was pastor, the church added the name St. John. The present building dates from 1892-93.

The first jail in Frankfort was on the northwest corner of the Old Statehouse Square. By the 1820s, the jail moved to this corner site. It was here on the site of the church in 1825 that Jereboam Beauchamp was held prisoner following the assassination of Solomon P. Sharp. The murder inspired several writings, including Edgar Allen Poe's *Politian* and Robert Penn Warren's *World Enough and Time*. The best factual account is *The Beauchamp-Sharp Tragedy* by J. Winston Coleman Jr. When Beauchamp and his wife realized he would hang for the crime, they decided to cheat the hangman by killing themselves. After a botched effort at poisoning, they stabbed themselves with a knife his wife Ann had smuggled into the cell. She died from the self-inflicted stabbing and Beauchamp, bleeding from his own wound, met his death at the gallows on Glens Creek Road. At their request, the two lay buried together arm and arm in the same coffin in Bloomfield, Kentucky's Maple Grove Cemetery. Today the body of Colonel Sharp lies in a grave near Daniel Boone in the Frankfort Cemetery. When President James Madison learned of the assassination, he referred to Solomon P. Sharp as having had one of the greatest minds west of the Alleghenies.

Achilles Sneed House CIRCA 1820 — 124 CLINTON STREET

Achilles Sneed was one of Frankfort's early businessmen and politicians. Sneed was born in Spotsylvania County, Virginia, and was a property holder in Frankfort as early as 1797. In 1805 Thomas Todd appointed Sneed to be the state's second Clerk of the Court of Appeals. Sneed also wrote Frankfort's first bestseller: *Decisions of the Court of Appeals of the State of Kentucky, 1801-1805*. It was popular because of widespread land litigation at the time. In 1807 he was a director of the Bank of Kentucky. He died in Frankfort in 1825. One of his daughters married U. S. Navy Commodore William S. Harris who was associated with the S. I. M. Major house on the northeast corner of Ann and Mero Streets.

Sneed was one of the original Frankfort Water Company incorporators along with Liberty Hall's John Brown and William Trigg in 1805. Workers stretched wooden pipes from Cedar Cove Spring into town. They created a reservoir by building a wall 25 feet high below the spring. The pipes used were cedar logs bored through the center and fastened to each other, end to end, with wooden pins. The water system was in use until 1886. In 1818 Sneed built a water gristmill at the Falls of Big Benson later known as Conway's mill. In 1822 he was appointed by the Franklin County Court as one of the commissioners to rebuild the county jail at the present site of the St. John AME Church on the northeast corner of Lewis and Clinton Street.

Sneed built the house around 1820. The original design was Federal style in Flemish bond brick. The Ann Street side of the home featured a fanlight-topped entrance, altered and enlarged later in the century. Sneed would sell the property to Colonel Thomas A. Theobald. The next owner, Mrs. Arabella Welch, turned the property into a boarding house following the sale of her Versailles Road farm. Later Eudora Lindsey South would turn that Versailles Road farm into the educational facility known as "Excelsior Institute." When Mrs. Welch died in 1878 Dr. Edgar Erskine Hume bought the house, renovating it into two dwellings fronting both Ann and Clinton Streets.

The latter 1820s found the Commonwealth of Kentucky in turmoil. Victims of the Panic of 1819 and the succeeding depression brought on by the War of 1812, were in need of relief from their debts. The legislature passed numerous measures designed to aid those in debt, but the Kentucky Court of Appeals found many of the measures unconstitutional. In a referendum held in 1824 the people of Kentucky voted in favor of relief. Statewide the pro-relief side captured a two-thirds majority in both legislative houses, which brought about the removal of the anti-relief judges referred to as the "Old Court." In a legislative session on Christmas Eve that year, the pro-relief forces were successful in getting passage of a court reorganization bill that eliminated the Old Court, creating a "New Court." In 1825 the Old Court refused to evacuate its offices or give up its records. In February of that year, New Court Clerk, Francis Preston Blair, forcefully entered the office of Old Court Clerk Achilles Sneed and removed the records. For his failure to comply with the court ruling to turn over the records, Sneed was fined ten pounds. In 1826, the legislature abolished the New Court and reinstated the Old Court. Blair later moved to Washington, and purchased a residence across from the White House. Today the Blair House is a special residence to house dignitaries who visit the President of the United States.

Achilles Sneed was buried in the Innes-Todd graveyard near Peaks Mill.

The most famous person associated with this house is artist Robert Burns Wilson. Born in Pennsylvania in 1850 and educated in Wheeling, West Virginia, he studied art in Pittsburgh, eventually moving to Louisville around 1872.

Achilles Sneed House

Here Robert Burns Wilson wrote Remember the Maine, the Battle Hymn of the Spanish-American War.

His portraits of prominent people in Louisville prompted *Kentucky Yeoman* editor S. I. M. Major and others to bring him to Frankfort in 1875. Here Wilson found a lucrative position doing local portraits in oil, crayon, and charcoal. He confined most of his landscapes to watercolors of the Kentucky River and Elkhorn Creek. During the 1880s his exhibitions were successful in both Louisville and New Orleans. He also attained fame through his writing. He published three books on poetry and a novel, *Until the Day Break*. Most of the action of his novel was set in "Harringford House," using as his model the Vest-Lindsey home at the southwest corner of Wapping and Washington Streets. The novel's principal story takes place in Frankfort. In 1953 Willard Rouse Jillson published *Romance and Reality, Notes and Identifications of Locale and Characters in Robert Burns Wilson's Novel: Until the Day Break*. Wilson's poem, Remember the Maine, his most noted work, was written in this house on Clinton Street in 1898 shortly after the battleship *U.S.S. Maine* was sunk in

Sigmund Luscher House

Havana Harbor. The poem set to music became the United States battle song of the Spanish-American War.

Wilson first lived in the Hanna House that stood at the southeast corner of Second and Conway streets opposite the southern end of today's Singing Bridge. When he dwelt here on Clinton Street, it was a boarding house belonging to Miss Lucy Ware. He once had a combined studio and sleeping room in Doctor Neville Garret's house at 207 West Second Street. Wilson lived for a time at 217 East Todd Street and in the old Drane house that stood at the west end of today's Second Street School.

Wilson fell in love with Frankfort's Belle Hensley, but she would marry someone else before he gained the financial stability to ask for her hand in marriage. In 1901at age 50, he married 20 year-old Anne Hendricks, the daughter of Kentucky's Attorney General Jack Hendricks who lived at Glenarry Farm on Versailles Road. Following a wedding in New York, they resided at 417 West Fourth Street in Frankfort. A daughter, Anne Elizabeth, was born in November of 1902 while they lived at this address. The family then moved to Brooklyn two years later.

In 1916, at age 65, Wilson suffered a heart attack, dying in obscurity in a Brooklyn hospital. Robert Burns Wilson is buried near Daniel Boone in the Frankfort Cemetery high above the Kentucky River he loved so well.

Sigmund Luscher House CIRCA 1869 — CLINTON STREET BETWEEN ANN AND HIGH STREETS

Swiss immigrant Sigmund Luscher was born in 1833. He opened a brewery in Frankfort on the east side of Ann Street in the late 1860s. The house Luscher built in 1869 originally stood at the north end of Ann Street near his brewery. With the anticipated construction of the Department of Transportation headquarters along Mero Street, his home was moved to this location on Clinton Street in 2001. At one time you could have bought this building for just $1.00, but there was a catch. The new owner would have to pay for the cost of moving the building, over $300,000! No one made any offers, so state officials accepted a project bid of $330,000 from Edwards Moving of Simpsonville. With the use of hydraulics and 128 wheels, they moved the house, re-routing traffic several hours in mid-October, 2001.

The house is on the National Register of Historic Places and is a wonderful example of Italianate architecture. In the early 1980s during renovation work, a former owner determined the brick walls to be of triple thickness. At the time he purchased the house, trees were growing through the roof and water damage had destroyed most of the original plasterwork.

In June of 1880 Sig Luscher started an ice manufacturing company at his brewery. Colonel T. L. Rankin's $10,000 ice machine, with a capacity of producing 20,000 pounds of ice a day, was one of the greatest inventions at that time. The *Kentucky Yeoman* newspaper wrote of Luscher's enterprise: "A few such men as Luscher are worth more to a community than millions of money in idle hands. The ice is in solid clear blocks, from six to eight inches thick and will last much longer than natural ice."

Sigmund Luscher died in 1891 and is buried in the Frankfort Cemetery.

The following anecdote is from Maurice H. Thatcher's *Stories and Speeches of William O. Bradley*. Bradley, Kentucky's first Republican Governor, gathered many humorous stories from his days as a lawyer. He tells this story on Luscher:

> "Sig Luscher was the proprietor of a brewery in Frankfort, Kentucky. In a case pending, a witness had testified that although he had drunk 14 glasses of beer during the day, he was thoroughly at himself at the time he witnessed the transaction concerning which he testified. Several physicians had testified as experts that the witness, in their judgment, could not have been free from intoxication, but, on the contrary, must have been in a confused state of mind.
>
> The attorney, desiring to sustain his witness, called Luscher to the stand, who testified that he had drunk beer daily from his earliest recollection; had for several years worked in a brewery, and for 10 years had been engaged in the manufacture of beer; that during all this time he had seen a large number of men drink beer;

Swiss emigrant Sig Luscher operated a brewery in Frankfort in the 1860s.

and that he knew he could state with certainty the amount of beer necessary to intoxicate.

The court ruled the witness competent, whereupon, the question was asked:

"Now, Mr. Luscher, from your experience as detailed, please tell the jury whether 14 glasses of beer drunk at intervals during the day, would seriously, or otherwise, affect the body or mind of the individual who drank it?"

"Vell," replied the witness, "ven I gets up mit te morning I trink haf tuzzen pottles pefore preakfast. Den, I sits down at te table and trink six pottles, and at tinner I trink ten pottles. Den, after tinner I trink six pottles, and at supper I trinks six more pottles, and it does not make me trunk, or even affect my mind a leetle pit. I tells you, shentlemen, no man will git trunk on peer unless he makes a tampt hog of himself."

First Baptist Church CIRCA 1908 — 100 WEST CLINTON STREET

In Frankfort during the early 1800s, blacks and whites worshipped together without incident. African-Americans were encouraged to worship with whites. In September of 1832, the Frankfort Board of Trustees ruled that blacks should not be forbidden to worship separately. Attendance at the Lewis Street Baptist Church (later to become First Baptist on St. Clair) had grown to where whites and blacks were holding separate services in the same building. In the writings of Dr. E. E. Underwood, we find that blacks and whites were holding their own services with their own pastors starting in 1833. When the Lewis Street Church burned in 1867, an African-American branch of the Baptist church began to meet in various homes. One church, called the "Colored Baptist Church," was located south of the penitentiary on the east extension of Clinton known as Shelby Street. John Ward, a free black property owner and Ziah Black donated land for a church building. Many blacks were still worshipping in the white Baptist church when the new structure on St. Clair was built in 1868. Another black group, "The First Independent Colored Baptist Church," met in the U. S. Freedman's Bureau School on Clinton Street. The church relocated to Mero, between St. Clair and Washington Streets. It would change its name to The Corinthian Baptist Church in 1893. In the 1960s when the Capital Plaza was developed, the Urban Renewal Agency purchased the property and the church then built a new facility in south Frankfort.

In 1894 the Clinton Street "Colored" First Baptist Church raised funds for a new building and money was placed in reserve for the purchase of another lot. The church relocated to its present site on the northwest corner of Clinton and High Streets. There was some protest that the church might be too close to the Governor's Mansion on the opposite corner. Frankfort officials attempted to halt construction by ignoring the petition of the church trustees for a building permit. When excavation began without the permit, authorities arrested the contractor, the church trustees and the workers. The local judge found them guilty and they were all assessed fines. In order to levy the fines, the Frankfort city council had to pass an additional ordinance.

The Clinton Street First Baptist Church trustees were determined to erect a new building. A temporary injunction was obtained to stop the city from interfering with the construction of a house of worship. In 1903 Judge James E. Cantrell dissolved the injunction by declaring "a Negro church is a 'nuisance' per se." The church trustees then took the case to the Court of Appeals where, in 1904, the decision was reversed and a perpetual injunction was granted. Ermina Jett Darnell in her colorful account on Frankfort, *Filling the Chinks*, writes:

"…Old Judge White routed the opponents completely, saying that it was the first time in his life that he had heard the Church of God denounced as a nuisance."

In the ruling on the case, the Court stated, "It would be strange indeed, to find it announced in the law books or declared by any court of final resort, that a beer garden or dance hall may exist in a city, yet a brick, fireproof church may not be erected therein…"

First Baptist Church

*The congregation had to go
to court in order to open their
church located across from
the Governors' Mansion in the
early 1900s.*

FIRST
BAPTIST
CHURCH

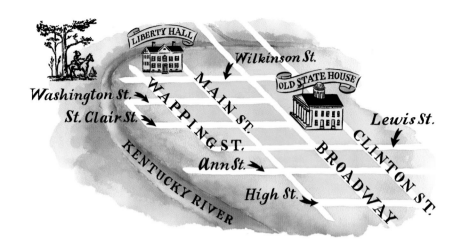

Chapter Ten
HIGH STREET

High Street runs from the Kentucky River north to the bottom of Fort Hill. The street was at the eastern "high" end of north Frankfort. A portion of the street where it intersected with Montgomery (Main) Street was somewhat elevated. At the time when Frankfort reached statehood in 1792, Clinton Street ended at the eastern intersection of High Street. A 1939 preliminary map of early Frankfort, 1786 to 1800, by Bayless Hardin, shows a Shelby Street going in a northeasterly direction past the southern side of the Frankfort Penitentiary. Shelby Street would later become an extension of Clinton Street. There are not many historic buildings remaining on High Street today. The 1840s Barstow House is now part of the Kentucky History Center and the State Office Building replaced the flood-ravaged prison in the late 1930s. The most significant structure is the 1798 Governor's Mansion that now serves as a home for the Lieutenant Governor of Kentucky.

Barstow House CIRCA 1845 — KENTUCKY HISTORY CENTER ON HIGH STREET

Michael Barstow was born in Yorkshire, England. He and his younger brother Jeremiah arrived in the United States in 1821. On the boat trip over, Jeremiah married his young sweetheart, Eleanor Peace Collette. In the 1840s businessman Michael Barstow bought this lot for $1,200. Barstow was among the very first members of the Church of Ascension on Washington Street. He ran a combination grocery and dry goods store located on the northeast corner of St. Clair and Broadway now the site of Serafini's Restaurant. The Barstow brothers also ran a local theatre on the second floor. When the life-long bachelor Barstow died in 1867, he left a portion of the property to the widow of his brother Jeremiah, Ellen P. Conery and her three children. One of the daughters, Mrs. Robert Jillson, took over the store and resided in one-half of the High Street duplex. Ellen had been married first to Jeremiah Barstow, then to General John Woods before marrying Auguste Conery. She was instrumental in the early development of the Catholic Church in Frankfort. In section G of the Frankfort Cemetery, there is a massive monument at her gravesite. Though "Helen" appears on the stone, her name is Eleanor.

The home, constructed on a cut stone foundation, is Frankfort's earliest duplex. Originally, the floor plan consisted of two large rooms and a hall on each of the three levels of each side. It has served as a residence, a boarding house and a rooming house. The building was remodeled in the 1900s. The right side is Italianate style, while the left side is representative of the Federal style. Several fires in recent years almost brought demolition to the structure. The City of Frankfort condemned the building in 1988 as part of an urban improvement project.

The three-story brick duplex is now an extension of the Kentucky History Center housing the Kentucky Historical Society's communications, marketing, publications and finance staff. The renovation of the historic duplex was at a cost of over $500,000.

"The Palace" (Old Governor's Mansion) CIRCA 1798 — 420 HIGH STREET

Between 1798 and 1914, this elegant mansion served as the home of 34 of Kentucky's early governors. Now the home for Kentucky's Lieutenant Governors, the structure is among the oldest official executive residences still in use in the United States, built three years before the White House. When Kentucky was admitted to the Union in 1792 there was no official residence for Isaac Shelby, Kentucky's first governor. He lived in a rented log house on the west end of Broadway. It was at his suggestion that the Legislature began building "The Palace." The Legislature appropriated 1,200 pounds and purchased the land from Thomas Todd, who married a sister of President James Madison's wife.

Thomas Metcalfe, one of the masons who laid the stone foundation for the building, would later himself reside in the house as Governor. Metcalfe's predecessor, Virginia blueblood Joseph Desha, kept him out of the mansion for several days because he was reluctant to give up the house to a common stonemason. Another story related in most of the early Frankfort histories holds that Governor Robert Perkins Letcher also helped lay the building's brick walls. If this is true, that would make him a very young brick mason, for Letcher, born in 1788, would have only been 10 years old at the time of the mansion's completion. Perhaps confusion was generated because Letcher's father, Stephen Giles Letcher, was the contractor for the brickwork. According to historian Lowell Harrison, in *The Kentucky Encyclopedia*, the Letcher family did not arrive in Kentucky until 1800, two years after the home was constructed.

The first to occupy the Mansion was Governor James Garrard, and the last was James B. McCreary. McCreary would serve a second term and be the first to live in the new Governor's Mansion in south Frankfort. While serving as Governor during the early 1800s, Charles Scott fell down the steps to the street and broke his hip. When he addressed the Kentucky troops going into the War of 1812, Scott, on crutches, became irate and savagely struck the steps saying "But for you, I would be going with these boys to fight for my country." Many political leaders who have helped to shape our country's history have visited the Mansion, including General William Henry Harrison, King Louis Phillipe of France, William Jennings Bryan, and President Teddy Roosevelt. President James Monroe and his aides Andrew Jackson and Zachary Taylor were here in 1819. President William Howard Taft came to Frankfort to dedicate the Lincoln statue in the Capitol Rotunda and was given an old fashioned Southern breakfast at the Mansion. The stone steps leading to the front door are the same steps that Lafayette climbed when he visited Frankfort in 1825.

Visitors include William Henry Harrison, French King Louis Phillipe, William Jennings Bryan, Teddy Roosevelt, James Monroe, Andrew Jackson, Zachary Taylor, Lafayette, and William Howard Taft.

The steps, the exterior brick and stairway paneling are thought to be the only original parts remaining in use. The interior experienced severe damage by fire in 1899. The house has gone through several extensive renovations during its history. It was originally built in both Georgian and Federal designs. In the mid-1800s an ornate cast iron Victorian porch graced the front door of the house. In 1859 the mansion was extensively renovated and builder John Haly was paid $690 to refurbish 23 windows and other areas of the Mansion were extensively refurbished. In 1868 came new gas light fixtures, draperies, carpeting and furniture. In 1910 the New State Capitol was built in south Frankfort, and a new Governor's Mansion was erected in 1914. The Old Mansion then remained vacant for several years. In 1938 the old iron porch was removed and other renovations were made so the State Highway Patrol might use the facility as barracks for state troopers. By 1946, the Old Mansion was declared unsafe and condemned. Simeon Willis, Kentucky's Governor at the time, gained support from the legislature and appropriated funds for restoration.

Today Mansion visitors can see the gold and pearl pen used to sign the executive order. Restoration work would continue for nearly ten years. After serving as a museum and a tourist attraction, the Old Mansion became the official residence of the state's lieutenant governors. Harry Lee Waterfield was the first to occupy the home. Lt. Governor Steve Henry and his wife, the former Miss America, Heather French Henry, became the proud parents of a daughter, Harper, in 2001. It was the first child born to a couple in the Old Governor's Mansion since Governor John Crepps Wickliffe Beckham and his wife, Jean Raphael Fuqua Beckham, had a baby daughter Eleanor Raphael in 1901.

"The Palace" (Old Governor's Mansion)

Bibliography

Alexander, Holmes. *Aaron Burr, The Proud Pretender.* NY: Harper & Brothers, 1937.

Baldwin, Leland D., and Robert Kelley. *The Stream of American History.* NY: American Book Company, 1965.

Bamberg, Robert D., Editor. *The Confession of Jereboam O. Beauchamp.* Philadelphia: University of Pennsylvania Press, 1966.

Brown, John Mason. *An Address Delivered on the Occasion of the Centennial Commemoration of the Town of Frankfort, Kentucky, October 6, 1886.* Louisville: Kentucky Lithograph and Printing Company, 1886.

Bryant, Ron. *Kentucky History, An Annotated Bibliography.* Westport, CT: Greenwood Press, 2000.

Carpenter, John W., and William B. Scott. *Kentucky Courthouses.* London, KY: 1988.

Casto, Marilyn. *Actors, Audiences, & Historic Theaters of Kentucky.* Lexington: The University Press of Kentucky, 2000.

Chinn. George Morgan. *Kentucky, Settlement and Statehood, 1750-1800.* Frankfort, KY: Kentucky Historical Society, 1975.

Clark, Jerry E. *The Shawnee.* Lexington: The University Press of Kentucky, 1993.

Coleman, Mrs. Chapman. *The Life of John J. Crittenden, Volumes I and II.* Philadelphia: J. P. Lippincott & Company, 1871.

Coleman Jr., J. Winston. *Famous Kentucky Duels,* Lexington, KY: Henry Clay Press, 1969.

_____. *Historic Kentucky,* Lexington, KY: Henry Clay Press, 1968.

_____. *The Beauchamp-Sharp Tragedy,* Frankfort, KY: Roberts Printing Company, 1950.

_____. *Lafayette's Visit to Lexington.* Lexington, KY: Winburn Press, 1969.

_____. *Robert Burns Wilson, Kentucky Painter, Novelist and Poet.* Lexington, KY: Winburn Press, 1956.

_____. *Stage-Coach Days in the Bluegrass.* Louisville: Standard Press, 1935.

Collins, Lewis and Richard H. *History of Kentucky Volumes I and II.* Frankfort: Kentucky Historical Society, 1966.

Colonial Dames of America. *Antiques in Kentucky,* Reprinted from The Magazine *Antiques.* March and April, 1974.

Curl, James Stevens. *A Dictionary of Architecture.* NY: Oxford University Press, 2000.

Darnell, Ermina Jett. *After the Manner of the Oak, a Study of the Growth of the Frankfort Christian Church.* Frankfort, KY: n.p., 1935.

_____. *Filling the Chinks,* Roberts Printing Company. Frankfort, KY: 1966.

_____. *South Frankfort, Kentucky.* Frankfort, KY: Roberts Printing Company, 1947.

Davis, William C. *Breckinridge: Statesman, Soldier, Symbol.* Baton Rouge: LSU Press, 1974.

Dugan, Frances L. S. and Jacqueline P. Bull, Editors. *Bluegrass Craftsman, Being the Reminiscences of Ebenezer Hiram Stedman Papermaker 1808-1885.* Lexington: University Press of Kentucky, 1959.

Elliott, Ron. *Assassination at the State House.* Kuttawa, KY: McClanahan Publishing House, 1995.

Everman, H.E. "Hank." *Governor James Garrard.* KY: Cooper's Run Press, 1981.

Faragher, John Mack. *Daniel Boone.* NY: Henry Holt and Company, 1992.

Farmers Bank and Capital Trust Company. *A Second Century of Progress with Frankfort.* Frankfort, KY: 1971.

Franklin County Bicentennial Edition. The Frankfort *State Journal,* May 7, 1995.

Glenn, Nettie. *Early Frankfort Kentucky, 1786-1861.* Frankfort, KY: 1986.

_____. *"Love to All, your Paul."* Ephrata, PA: Science Press, 1974.

Goff, John S., "The Last Leaf: George Mortimer Bibb," *Register of the Kentucky Historical Society* (October 1961), Frankfort, Kentucky.

Goin, Kenneth. *Captain Sanford W. Goin.* Frankfort, KY: unpublished 2000.

_____. *South Frankfort, Thirty-Eight Years A Town.* Frankfort, KY: 1972.

Hamel, Mary Michele. *A Kentucky Artist, Paul Sawyier (1865-1917).* Richmond, KY: The Fred P. Giles Gallery, Eastern Kentucky University, 1975.

Hardin, Bayless E., "The Brown Family of Liberty Hall," *The Filson Club History Quarterly,* Louisville, Kentucky, 1942.

_____. *Notebooks on Frankfort and Franklin County.* Frankfort, KY: unpublished, Kentucky Historical Society.

_____, "Dr. Preston W. Brown, 1775-1826," *The Filson Club Quarterly,* Louisville, Kentucky, 1945.

Hatter, Russell, *Notes on Frankfort and Franklin County, Kentucky,* unpublished.

Harrison, Lowell H. *The Civil War in Kentucky.* Lexington: The University Press of Kentucky, 1975.

_____. "Kentucky-Born Generals in the Civil War," *Register of the Kentucky Historical Society,* (April 1966).

_____., Editor. *Kentucky's Governors, 1792-1985.* Lexington: The University Press of Kentucky, 1985.

_____. *George Rogers Clark and the War in the West.* The University Press of Kentucky, Lexington, Kentucky, 1976.

Harrison, Lowell H., and James C. Klotter. *A New History of Kentucky.* Lexington: The University Press of Kentucky, 1997.

Herr, Kincaid A., *The Louisville and Nashville Railroad, 1850-1963.* Lexington: The University Press of Kentucky, 2000.

Hinds, Charles F. *Ascension Episcopal Church, Frankfort, Kentucky, 1836-1996.* Frankfort, KY: HAC, Inc., 1996.

_____. *History of First Baptist Church, Frankfort, Kentucky, 1816-1991.* Frankfort, KY: 1991.

Hockensmith, Charles D. *Bricks and Brick Making in Frankfort.* Frankfort, KY: Kentucky Heritage Council, 1996.

Hughes, Jr., Nathaniel Cheairs and Thomas Clayton Ware. *Theodore O'Hara.* Knoxville: The University of Tennessee Press, 1998.

Hughes, Nicky, "Fort Boone and the Civil War Defense of Frankfort," *The Register of the Kentucky Historical Society,* (Spring, 1990).

Hume, Edgar Erskine. *LaFayette in Kentucky.* Frankfort, KY: Transylvania College and The Society of Cincinnati in the State of Virginia, 1937.

Index of the Frankfort Cemetery. Frankfort, KY: 1999.

Jillson, Willard Rouse, "Aaron Burr's Trial for Treason, at Frankfort, 1806," *Filson Club History Quarterly* (October, 1943).

_____. *Early Frankfort and Franklin County, 1750-1850.* Louisville: The Standard Printing Company, 1936.

_____. *The First Landowners of Frankfort, Kentucky, 1774-1790.* Frankfort, KY: The *State Journal,* 1945.

_____. *Henry Clay's Defense of Aaron Burr in 1806.* Frankfort, KY: Roberts Printing Company, 1943.

_____. *A Historical Bibliography of Frankfort, Kentucky, 1751-1941.* Frankfort, KY: The State Journal Company, 1942.

_____. *Irvin S. Cobb at Frankfort, Kentucky.* Carrollton, KY: The News-Democrat Press, 1944.

_____. *Paul Sawyier and His Paintings.* Louisville: Standard Printing Company, Inc., 1965.

_____. *Paul Sawyier: American Artist (1865-1917).* Frankfort, KY: Bluegrass Press, Inc., 1971.

_____. *Romance and Reality, Notes and Identifications of Locale and Characters in Robert Burns Wilson's Novel: Until the Day Break.* Frankfort, KY: Roberts Printing Company, 1953.

_____. *Sketches of Early Frankfort, Kentucky.* Frankfort, KY: Roberts Printing Company, 1950.

_____. *Literary Haunts and Personalities of Old Frankfort, 1791-1941.* Frankfort, KY: The Kentucky Historical Society, 1941.

Johnson, Lewis Franklin. *Famous Kentucky Tragedies and Trials.* Louisville: Baldwin Law Book Company, 1916.

_____. *The History of Franklin County, Kentucky.* Frankfort, KY:

Roberts Printing Company, 1912.

_____. *History of the Franklin County Bar, 1786-1932.* Frankfort, KY: Frank K. Kavanaugh, 1932.

Jones, Arthur F. *The Art of Paul Sawyier.* Lexington: University Press of Kentucky, 1976.

Kallsen, Loren J., Editor. *The Kentucky Tragedy, A Problem in Romantic Attitude.* NY: The Bobbs-Merrill Company, Inc. 1963.

Kentucky's Black Heritage. Frankfort, KY: Kentucky Commission on Human Rights, 1971.

Kleber, John E., Editor in Chief. *The Encyclopedia of Louisville.* Lexington, KY: The University Press of Kentucky, 2001.

_____. *The Kentucky Encyclopedia,* Lexington: The University Press of Kentucky, 1992.

Kirwan, Albert D. *John J. Crittenden.* Lexington: University Press of Kentucky, 1962.

Klotter, James C. *The Breckinridges of Kentucky, 1760-1981.* Lexington: The University Press of Kentucky, 1986.

_____. *William Goebel, The Politics of Wrath.* Lexington, KY: The University Press of Kentucky, 1977.

Kramer, Carl E. *Capital on the Kentucky.* Frankfort, KY: Historic Frankfort, Inc., 1986.

Lancaster, Clay. *Antebellum Architecture of Kentucky.* Lexington: The University Press of Kentucky, 1991.

Leckie, Robert. *George Washington's War.* NY: Harper/Collins, 1992.

Liberty Hall-1796, Orlando Brown House-1835. Frankfort, KY: Colonial Dames of America, 1989.

Martin, James Kirby. *Benedict Arnold, Revolutionary Hero, An American Warrior Reconsidered.* NY: New York University Press, 1997.

McCready, Richard Lightburne. *The Church of the Ascension, Frankfort, Kentucky,* 1939.

Meagher, Paul F. *The Centennial Celebration of the Church of the Good Shepard, Frankfort, Kentucky, 1848-1948.* Frankfort, KY: Perry Publishing Company, 1948.

Olcott, Sara Prewitt and T. E. Adams. *Historical Jottings of Kentucky's Capital.* Frankfort, KY: 1951.

Parrish, William E. *Frank Blair, Lincoln's Conservative.* Columbia, MO: University of Missouri Press, 1998.

Pruett, Rebecca K. *The Browns of Liberty Hall.* Frankfort, KY: The National Society of Colonial Dames of America, 1966.

Ramage, James A. *Rebel Raider, The Life of General John Hunt Morgan.* Lexington: The University Press of Kentucky, 1986.

Robertson, James I. *Stonewall Jackson, The Man, The Soldier, The Legend.* NY: Macmillan Publishing USA, 1997.

Russell, Francis. *The Shadow of Blooming Grove, Warren G. Harding in His Times.* NY: McGraw-Hill Book Company, 1968.

Saddlebags to Steeples: A Heritage of Methodism in Frankfort, Kentucky.

Frankfort, KY: First United Methodist Church, 1985.

Schmidt, Martin F. *Kentucky Illustrated, The First Hundred Years.* Lexington: The University Press of Kentucky, 1992.

Scott, Robert W., edited by Thomas D. Clark. *Footloose in Jacksonian America, Robert W. Scott and his Agrarian World.* Frankfort, KY: The Kentucky Historical Society, 1989.

Short, Jim. *Caleb Powers and The Mountain Army.* Olive Hill, KY: Jessica Publishing, 1997.

Smith, Gerald L. *A Black Educator in the Segregated South, Kentucky's Rufus B. Atwood.* Lexington: The University Press of Kentucky, 1994.

Sower, Frank W., *Reflections on Frank fort 1751-1900.* Frankfort, KY: 1994.

Sprague, Stuart and Elizabeth Perkins. *Frankfort, A Pictorial History.* Virginia Beach, VA: Donning Company, 1980.

Staples, Charles R. *The History of Pioneer Lexington, 1779-1806.* Lexington: The University Press of Kentucky, 1996.

Steers, Jr., Edward. *Blood on the Moon, The Assassination of Abraham Lincoln.* Lexington: The University Press of Kentucky, 2001.

Stucker, Agnes Catherine. *The Carneal-Watson House, 405-407 Wapping Street, Frankfort, Kentucky.* N.p., n.d.

Tapp, Hamilton, and James C. Klotter. *Kentucky: Decades of Discord, 1865-1900.* Frankfort, KY: The Kentucky Historical Society, 1977.

Trabue, Alice Elizabeth. *A Corner in Celebrities.* Louisville: The Filson Club, 1958.

Warner, Ezra J. *Generals in Blue.* Baton Rouge: LSU Press, 1988.

_____. *Generals in Gray.* Baton Rouge: LSU Press, 1988.

Warren, Robert Penn. *World Enough & Time.* Vintage Books, 1979.

Wells, Dianne and Mary Lou S. Madigan. *Update: Guide to Kentucky Historical Highway Markers.* Frankfort, KY: Kentucky Historical Society, 1983.

Willis, George Lee. *History of Shelby County, Kentucky.* Baltimore: Clearfield Company, 1999.

_____. *Willard Rouse Jillson; A Biographical Sketch.* Louisville: The Standard Printing Company Inc., 1930.

Woodson, Mary Willis. *Through the Portals of Glen Willis.* Frankfort, KY: Franklin County Trust for Historic Preservation.

Woodson, Urey. *First New Dealer.* Louisville: The Standard Press, 1939.

Index